McKinley Bibliographies

BLACK STUDIES: A BIBLIOGRAPHY

For the Use of Schools,
Libraries and the General Reader

Compiled by
LEONARD B. IRWIN

McKinley Publishing Co.
Brooklawn, N. J.
1973

S B N 910942-02-1

Printed in the United States
by

CLARK PRINTING HOUSE, INC.
PHILADELPHIA, PENNSYLVANIA

TO JESS

Who suggested this topic

TABLE OF CONTENTS

INTRODUCTION

One of the more notable developments in education in the past decade has been the recognition that ethnic minorities as a significant part of American life have been largely neglected. Traditionally, school curricula in the humanities tended to treat American history and culture as an entity dominated by white standards and backgrounds derived from their sources in classical and western Europe. Little effort was made to bring home to children and young students the fact that a considerable proportion of our population was made up of Negroes, Mexicans, Puerto Ricans, Indians, Orientals and eastern Europeans, whose roots, cultures and problems were quite different from those of the majority. Not until quite recently have educators and publishers seriously come to realize that the courses and teaching materials they provided had little relevance to these ethnic minorities. We had been teaching about a so-called democratic way of life while almost totally ignoring the existence of a large part of the population. The art, literature, music and social history that dominated our teaching were almost entirely those that had come to us basically through our British background, and with which our minority groups had no sense of participation.

Events of the past few years have shaken the social fabric of the nation to the roots, and one of their effects has been to make our educational system aware of its lack of communication with ethnic groups that form a large part of its clientele. Particularly has this been true concerning the black minority, which forms the oldest, largest and perhaps the most dissatisfied ethnic group. Schools in a number of cities and states have more Negro than white pupils; and most colleges and universities have significant numbers of black students. Willingly or not, curriculum makers have found it necessary to amend or add to their offerings in the social subjects material directly related to the background and current interests of blacks. In many cases new material has been incorporated into existing courses; in other instances, new courses of "black studies" have been set up. Either way, it has been necessary to re-train teachers and to provide new books and teaching aids for the students. As a result, hundreds of books have appeared on the market in the past decade or so, presenting every aspect of Negro history, thought and culture. The present volume has been designed as a guide to this literature in the hope that libraries and teachers will find it helpful in an area not hitherto very familiar to them.

The book is divided into five sections. The first part lists works dealing primarily with the history of black people in America from the earliest days to the present. The second part contains titles of a more personal nature, — biographies, autobiographies and memoirs where the emphasis is on individuals. The third section lists books whose purpose is primarily expository or analytical, expressing opinions and reactions to the racial situation. Part IV lists books dealing with various aspects of Negro culture and achievements in the arts. The last section includes some titles dealing with African history and development, works of reference, and subjects that do not readily fall in the previous categories.

No attempt has been made to include works of fiction by or about black people, except for a few anthologies of short stories. Textbooks also have generally been omitted. With these exceptions, the compiler has tried to include listings of as many books as possible dealing with Negroes, of a kind that may be useful to teachers, general readers and students of various age levels. Except for a few very significant titles, all the books listed have been published within the past twenty years, most within the last decade. It goes without saying that good books about race have been written in earlier years, but this is a subject where currency is particularly important.

Nearly all titles are accompanied by a brief descriptive annotation. Also each title is preceded by a letter symbol indicating the main interest level of the book:

(A) For general adult reading, teacher background, or mature students.

(Y) For young people; high school level.

(J) For student reading generally from grades six to ten.

Many of the books listed are currently available in paperback editions, and are so indicated by the word "paper" following date of publication. Such editions may not necessarily be issued under the original publisher's name, but this kind of information is, of course, easily obtained from the usual reference sources.

It is the compiler's hope that this bibliography will be helpful to (1) librarians seeking suitable titles to put on their shelves; (2) teachers looking for supplementary material for their classes, or for their own enrichment; and (3) for students needing guidance in research. Recognition of the importance of the Negro in the life of America is not a passing educational fad; and it will continue to be a serious subject for study and thought in the years to come.

SYMBOLS USED IN THIS WORK

(A) For general adult reading, teacher background, or mature students.

(Y) For young people; high school level.

(J) For student reading generally from grades six to ten.

PART I

HISTORY OF THE BLACK EXPERIENCE IN AMERICA

(A) Abrams, Charles. *Forbidden neighbors; a study of prejudice in housing.* Harper, 1955.
An important and authoritative book, especially for its time, written by a leading official in the field of housing. General library use.

(A) Aitken, Hugh G. J. (ed.) *Did slavery pay? Readings in the economics of black slavery in the United States.* Houghton, 1971. Paper.
A source for students of black history.

(Y) Alvarez, Joseph. *From reconstruction to revolution.* Atheneum, 1971.
For teen-agers, a history of the black effort for equal rights since the Civil War. A good survey.

(A,Y) Anthony, Earl. *Picking up the gun: a report on the Black Panthers.* Dial, 1970.
An account of the beginnings of the Black Panther organization, by one of its early leaders. Background reading.

(A) Aptheker, Herbert. *American Negro slave revolts.* International Publishers, 1943. Paper.
Scholarly research explaining in detail the causes of slave insurrections, and describing many of them, indicating that "slave docility" was not nearly as normal as tradition has had it. Good basic resource on this topic. Subjective but well-documented.

(A) Aptheker, Herbert (ed.) *A documentary history of the Negro people in the United States from colonial times through the Civil War.* Citadel, 1951, 1963. Paper.
Two volumes of speeches, petitions and letters by Negroes from colonial days on. Best collection of early Negro writings.

1

(A) Aptheker, Herbert. *Essays in the history of the American Negro.* International Publishers, 1945, 1964. Paper.
Four essays on slave revolts and on Negro participation in the Revolution, the abolitionist movement and the Civil War. Strongly sympathetic.

(A) Ardrey, Robert. *African genesis.* Atheneum, 1962. Paper.
Highly readable, somewhat sensational and very controversial summary of evidence showing that man evolved in Africa a half-million years ago.

(A) Ashmore, Harry S. *The Negro and the schools.* Univ. of North Carolina Press, 1964. Paper.
The Negro in education since emancipation.

(A) Aukofer, Frank A. *City with a chance.* Bruce Pub. Co., 1968.
A reporter's first-hand account of the civil rights and open housing troubles in Milwaukee in 1967.

(A) Bardolph, Richard (ed.) *The civil rights record; black Americans and the law, 1849-1970.* Crowell, 1970. Paper.
Very thorough collection of 500 pertinent documents — legislative, judicial and administrative. Good connecting material by the editor. An excellent source book for any black studies course.

(A) Barnes, Gilbert H. *The anti-slavery impulse, 1830-1844.* Peter Smith, 1933, 1957. Paper.
Serious work of history, good for adult reading and research.

(A,Y) Bayliss, John F. (ed.) *Black slave narratives.* Collier Books, 1970. Paper.
Good collection for reference or supplementary reading. Any level.

(A,Y) Bennett, Lerone, Jr. *Before the Mayflower; a history of the Negro in America, 1619-1962.* Johnson Pub. Co., 1969. Rev. Ed. Paper.
An easily-read history of 330 pages, plus a fifty-page chronological outline of significant events. The emphasis throughout is strongly sympathetic to the Negro, but is fair. Good for general reading, any library.

2

(A,Y) Bennett, Lerone, Jr. *Black power, U.S.A.; the human side of reconstruction, 1867-1877.* Johnson Pub. Co., 1967. Paper.

Interesting account of the Reconstruction period by a Negro historian. Useful for school library lists, as it gives a different view from most white accounts.

(A,Y) Bennett, Lerone, Jr. *Confrontation; black and white.* Johnson Pub. Co., 1965. Paper.

Good general history of Negro struggle and rebellion during the past three centuries in America. Useful for college or high school reading.

(A) Berger, Monroe. *Equality by statute; the revolution in civil rights.* Doubleday, 1967. Paper.

A scholarly survey of the history and efficacy of government attempts to protect civil rights by law.

(A,Y) Bergman, Peter M. *Chronological history of the Negro in America.* Harper, 1969. Paper.

Useful reference, with many readable sections of little-known information. For any library. Excellent index.

(A) Berry, Mary F. *Black resistance/white law.* Appleton, 1971. Paper.

A history of the black experience in America; the basic theme is that white society has always used constitutional and legalistic means to suppress the Negro.

(A) Bittle, William E. and Gilbert Geis. *The longest way home.* Wayne State Univ. Press, 1964.

History of an early twentieth century attempt by a group of Negroes to establish a black community in frontier Oklahoma and later to migrate to Africa.

(A) Blaustein, Albert P. and Clarence Ferguson. *Desegregation and the law; the meaning and effect of the school segregation cases.* Rutgers Univ. Press, 1957.

A good analysis and background study of the *Brown v. Topeka Board of Education* decision. Useful for teacher and general adult reading.

(A) Blaustein, Albert P. and R. Zangrando (eds.) *Civil rights and the American Negro*. Trident, 1968. Paper.

Collection of about one hundred documents dealing with Negro rights over the past three centuries: legal decisions, speeches, government documents and other items. Excellent as reference source.

(A) Bloch, Herman D. *The circle of discrimination*. New York Univ. Press, 1969.

A history of the discrimination against blacks in New York City since colonial times. Scholarly, useful for adult research on how these conditions arise.

(A,Y) Blossom, Virgil T. *It has happened here*. Harper, 1959.

Very readable account of the Little Rock, Arkansas, school integration crisis in 1957, written by the then Superintendent of Schools who was in the center of the storm. For any public or school library.

(J) Bontemps, Arna. *Story of the Negro*. Knopf, 1962.

History of black people, beginning in Africa and spreading overseas, to about 1954. Includes a useful chronology. For intermediate grades.

(A,Y) Bontemps, Arna and Jack Conroy. *Anyplace but here*. Hill & Wang, 1966.

Interesting history of Negro migration from the South to Northern cities over the years, and of many personalities and events. Good popular-type reading for any library.

(A) Bormann, Ernest G. (ed.) *Forerunners of Black Power; the rhetoric of abolition*. Prentice, 1971. Paper.

Contains fifteen notable speeches by leading abolitionists in the pre-Civil War period. The editor supplies historical and biographical material on each. Interesting examples of the fiery oratory that marked the abolition movement.

(A,Y) Botkin, Benjamin (ed.) *Lay my burden down; a folk history of slavery*. Univ. of Chicago Press, 1945. Paper.

Collection of slave narratives, a phase of the Federal Writers' Project of 1938. Interesting supplementary material for black history.

(A) Bracey, John H., August Meier and Elliott Rudwick (eds.) *Black nationalism in America*. Bobbs, 1970. Paper.

Collection of documents dealing with the history of the black nationalism movement since the 18th century. Valuable resource for larger libraries.

(A) Brawley, Benjamin. *Social history of the American Negro.* **Macmillan, 1921, reprinted by Johnson Pub. Co., 1968.**
A scholarly work, important for its time. A general history of slavery, with chapters on the West Indies and Liberia.

(A,Y) Breyfogle, William. *Make free: the story of the Underground Railroad.* **Lippincott, 1958.**
An interesting history, good for background reading for high school students or adults.

(A) Bridges, Hal. *Civil War and reconstruction.* **American Historical Assoc., 1957.**
A publication of the Service Center for Teachers of History, summarizing current historical conclusions.

(A) Brisbane, Robert. *The black vanguard.* **Judson, 1970. Paper.**
A descriptive history of black social movements and organizations, 1900-1960.

(J) Buckmaster, Henrietta. *Flight to freedom; the story of the Underground Railroad.* **Crowell-Collier, 1958. Paper.**
A good account of the subject for junior high school pupils.

(A,Y) Buckmaster, Henrietta. *Freedom bound.* **Macmillan, 1965. Paper.**
A history of the Reconstruction period for the general reader.

(A,Y) Buckmaster, Henrietta. *The Seminole wars.* **Collier, 1966.**
Good account of this long struggle which involved Negroes as well as Indians.

(A) Bullock, Paul (ed.) *Watts: the aftermath.* **Grove, 1969. Paper.**
A report on the Watts area of Los Angeles derived from interviews with its residents since the riots. Fair and interesting.

(A) Carlisle, Rodney P. *Prologue to liberation: a history of black people in America.* **Appleton, 1971.**
A history of the American Negro for the general reader.

(A) Cash, W. J. *The mind of the South.* **Random, 1960. Paper.**
About the ways of thinking prevalent in the South during and after the Civil War.

(Y) Chambers, Bradford (comp.) *Chronicles of Negro protest.* **Parents Magazine Press, 1968. Paper.**
Contains 42 documents of various kinds, in full or part, which are important in the Negro's history. Each is accompanied by a good introduction and explanation of its significance. Good material for school libraries.

(Y) Chapman, Abraham (ed.) *Steal away: stories of the runaway slaves.* **Praeger, 1971.**
Primarily for high school students, an anthology of fourteen excerpts from narratives by former slaves.

(Y) Cohen, Tom. *Three who dared.* **Doubleday, 1969. Paper.**
Very readable account of the experiences of three Northern civil rights workers, two white, one black, who went South to aid in the early days of the movement.

(Y) Commager, Henry S. *The great proclamation.* **Bobbs, 1960.**
A history of the Emancipation Proclamation, written for high school students.

(A) Conot, Robert. *Rivers of blood, years of darkness.* **Morrow, 1968. Paper.**
Highly detailed and vivid account of the causes and events of the Watts riot in Los Angeles. Valuable especially for exploring Negro conditions that can lead to such things.

(A) Conrad, Earl. *The invention of the Negro.* **Eriksson, 1966. Paper.**
A study of how the concept of racism grew and spread during American history. Deals chiefly with the pre-twentieth century period. Good analysis for general background.

(A) Cornish, Dudley. *The sable arm; Negro troops in the Union Army, 1861-1865.* **Norton, 1966. Paper.**
Specialized information for the general reader.

(A) Crowe, Charles (ed.) *Age of Civil War and Reconstruction, 1830-1900.* Dorsey, 1966. Paper.
Collection of outstanding essays by leading historians. Good for teachers and students of racial history.

(A) Cruden, Robert. *The Negro in Reconstruction.* Prentice, 1969. Paper.
Well-written and useful history of the meaning of the Reconstruction period to the blacks. College level.

(Y) Cuban, Larry. *The Negro in America.* Scott, Foresman, 1964. Paper.
A series of excerpts from various sources, grouped to illustrate fifteen problems of American Negro history, and accompanied by questions and study helps. For high school use.

(A) Curry, Richard O. and Joanna Cowden (eds.) *Slavery in America.* Peacock, 1972.
This is a reprinting, with considerable editorial addition, of Theodore Weld's noted anti-slavery book published in 1839. Useful for teacher background.

(A) Dann, Martin E. (ed.) *The black press 1827-1890: the quest for national identity.* Putnam, 1971.
Prefaced by an historical essay on black newspapers in the nineteenth century, this work is an anthology of excerpts from a number of them — articles on phases of the racial problem.

(A) Davidson, Basil. *Black mother; the years of the African slave trade.* Little, 1961.
One of the most interesting and authoritative studies of slavery in Africa and its relationships to America. Useful for general adult background reading.

(A) Davis, David B. *The problem of slavery in Western culture.* Cornell Univ. Press, 1966. Paper.
Sound and scholarly, dealing with the history and social aspects of slavery on a broad scale.

(A) Delany, M. R. and Robert Campbell. *Search for a place.* Univ. of Michigan Press, 1969.
Reprints of two separate books originally published in the late 1800's. The authors had gone to Nigeria in 1859-60 to determine the possibility of re-locating American Negroes there. This is a valuable source on early Negro separatist movements.

(A) Dennis, R. Ethel. *Black people of America — illustrated history.* Readers Press, 1970.

(A) Dillon, Merton. *Benjamin Lundy and the struggle for Negro freedom.* Univ. of Illinois Press, 1966.
Scholarly study of the abolitionist movement.

(A,Y) Dorman, Michael. *We shall overcome.* Delacorte, 1964. Paper.
Vivid eyewitness account of the critical events of 1962-63 in the South, particularly in Mississippi and Alabama. The author is a veteran Northern reporter, and this book is good journalism. It is easy to read and worthwhile history.

(A) Douglas, William O. *Mr. Lincoln and the Negroes.* Atheneum, 1963.
About Lincoln's beliefs concerning slavery and Negro equality. The book includes documents.

(A) Draper, Theodore. *Rediscovery of black nationalism.* Viking, 1970. Paper.
Critical study of the various back-to-Africa movements in American history. The author calls them a fantasy for both whites and blacks.

(A) Drimmer, Melvin (comp.) *Black history: a reappraisal.* Doubleday, 1968. Paper.
Contains about thirty excerpts from as many historians' writings on the Negro in America, from slavery to the present. There is an explanatory introduction to each section.

(Y) Drisko, Carol and Edgar Toppin. *The unfinished march.* Doubleday, 1967. Paper.
Negro history in America from the Reconstruction period to the First World War. Good for middle schools or slow secondary school readers.

(A) Duberman, Martin (ed.) *The anti-slavery vanguard: new essays on the abolitionists.* Princeton Univ. Press, 1965. Paper.
Seventeen essays, generally favorable, about this controversial group. Good background material for adults.

(A) DuBois, W. E. B. *Black reconstruction in America.* Russell, 1935, 1956. Paper.

An important book of over 700 pages. Extremely thorough and detailed history of the period from 1860 to 1880 as it concerned the Negro and his part in Reconstruction. The findings and point-of-view are quite different from those of most white historians of the period.

(A) DuBois, W. E. B. *The souls of black folk.* Fawcett, 1961. Paper.

Essays originally written in 1903. They try to show what it meant to be black between the Civil War and 1900. Good background for teachers.

(A) DuBois, W. E. B. *The world and Africa.* International Publishers Co., 1947. Paper.

Excellent review of the interrelationships of Africa and the European nations. Valuable teacher background.

(A) Duignan, Peter and Clarence Clendenen. *The United States and the African slave trade, 1619-1862.* Stanford Univ. Press, 1963.

An authoritative history of the subject.

(A) Dumond, Dwight L. *Anti-slavery: the crusade for freedom in America.* Univ. of Michigan Press, 1961. Paper.

Causes of the Civil War. Valuable in its analysis of the slavery problem and of its constitutional aspects.

(A) Dumond, Dwight L. *Anti-slavery origins of the Civil War in the United States.* Univ. of Michigan Press, 1959. Paper.

Scholarly historical work.

(J) Durham, Philip and Everett Jones. *Adventures of the Negro cowboys.* Dodd, 1966. Paper.

Written for juvenile readers and based on the authors' longer book, *The Negro Cowboys.*

(A,Y) Durham, Philip and Everett Jones. *The Negro cowboys.* Dodd, 1965.

Role of the Negro in the development of the West. Suitable for secondary school use.

(A) Eaton, Clement. *Growth of Southern civilization.* **Harper, 1963. Paper.**
Life in the ante-bellum South with stress on Negro resistance to slavery.

(A) Eaton, Clement. *A history of the Old South.* **Macmillan, 1949.**
One of the standard works on this subject.

(A) Elkins, Stanley M. *Slavery: a problem in American institutional and intellectual life.* **Grosset & Dunlap, 1963. Paper.**
How American slavery differed from other slave systems.

(A) Essien-Udom, E. U. *Black nationalism in America.* **Dell, 1962. Paper.**
A history of the Black Muslim movement.

(A) Feldstein, Stanley. *Once a slave.* **Morrow, 1970.**
A collection of reports written or told by slaves, mostly between 1830 and 1865, of what it was actually like to be a slave.

(A) Feldstein, Stanley (ed.) *The poisoned tongue; a documentary history of American racism and prejudice.* **Morrow, 1972. Paper.**
An interesting collection of 63 documents and excerpts, from all periods of American history, illustrating extreme racism against Negroes, Orientals, Jews, Catholics and foreigners generally. A good resource reader for this kind of material.

(A) Filler, Louis. *Crusade against slavery, 1830-1860.* **Harper (Torch Books), 1960. Paper.**
A history of abolitionism and slavery in politics.

(A) Fishel, Leslie and Benjamin Quarles (eds.) *The Negro American.* **Morrow, 1968. Paper.**
A collection of documents from many sources illustrating the history of the Negro from Africa to the present. Emphasis is mostly on earlier periods. Interesting and useful for students in school or for the general reader.

(A) Fitzhugh, George. *Cannibals all!* **(Edited by C. Vann Woodward.) Harvard Univ. Press, 1960. Paper.**
This is a reprint of a book originally published in 1857. The author was a Virginia planter and lawyer, who was convinced that the Southern slave system was far superior to Northern "wage slavery." The book was widely read and debated all over the country.

(A) Fladeland, Betty. *Men and Brothers: Anglo-American Antislavery Cooperation.* **Univ. of Illinois Pr., 1972.**
A scholarly study of the close relationships between abolitionists in England and the United States before the Civil War. A valuable addition to the history of slavery in an area not hitherto widely covered.

(A) Foner, Eric (comp.) *America's black past; a reader in Afro-American history.* **Harper, 1970. Paper.**
Primarily a reference source for teachers. Contains twenty-five selections from as many writers on the history and thinking of blacks. There are editorial introductions to each selection, and a good bibliography on black history.

(A) Franklin, John Hope. *The Emancipation Proclamation.* **Doubleday, 1963. Paper.**
A scholarly study for adult readers.

(A) Franklin, John Hope. *From slavery to freedom.* **2nd ed. Knopf, 1956. Paper.**
One of the standard works on the story of Negro and Caribbean Indian slavery. It is long and thorough, covering 650 pages. There is an exhaustive bibliography of references, up to about 1947. Not a book for light reading or for secondary students, but should be in every library.

(A,Y) Franklin, John Hope. *An illustrated history of black Americans.* **Time-Life Books, 1970.**
An attractive and easy-to-read book of Negro history. It is filled with excellent photographs. Very suitable for high school libraries.

(A) Franklin, John Hope. *The militant South.* **Beacon, 1964. Paper.**
A study of the thinking of the leaders of the South before the Civil War.

(A) Franklin, John Hope and Isidore Starr (comps.) *The Negro in twentieth century America*. Vantage, 1967. Paper.
Basic source material on the civil rights movement.

(A) Franklin, John Hope. *Reconstruction after the Civil War*. Univ. of Chicago, 1961. Paper.
Scholarly account of the role of blacks in reconstructed Southern governments.

(Y) Frazier, Edward Franklin. *The Negro in the United States*. Macmillan, 1965.
A survey history, especially useful for high school use.

(A,Y) Frazier, Thomas R. (ed.) *Afro-American history: primary sources*. Harcourt, 1971. Paper.
Anthology of writings by blacks, from slaves to present-day leaders like Carmichael. They are generally short, readable and interesting, and accompanied by questions and bibliographies. Suitable for secondary or college black studies courses.

(A) Frederickson, George. *The black image in the white mind*. Harper, 1971.
A serious survey of white American racial ideology during the 19th and early 20th century, and of the justificationss offered for anti-Negro attitudes.

(A) Freimark, Vincent and Bernard Rosenthal (eds.) *Race and the American romantics*. Schocken, 1971.
The most noted of 19th century American writers (Lowell, Poe, Whitman, etc.) were only lukewarm against slavery, at best. This is the theme of this anthology of writings about slavery by ten famous authors.

(A,Y) Fulks, Bryan. *Black struggle*. Delacorte, 1970.
Survey of the history of blacks in America. Good for general background reading, secondary school or above.

(A,Y) Furnas, J. C. *Goodbye to Uncle Tom*. Sloane, 1956. Paper.
Interesting and readable book about the Negro past and how his image of inferiority came to be. Much curious lore for teachers and older secondary school students, or the general reader.

(A) Furnas, J. C. *The road to Harpers Ferry.* Sloane, 1959.
A long book of 400 pages which tells, in colorful detail, the story of Negro slavery in Africa, the West Indies and in America; of the abolition movement, and in particular of Garrison and John Brown. Written in popular style for the general reader.

(A) Gara, Larry. *The Liberty Line: the legend of the Underground Railroad.* Univ. of Kentucky Press, 1961. Paper.
A scholarly study which attacks many of the generally-accepted myths, especially about a highly-organized abolitionist system of escape.

(A) Garrison, William Lloyd. *Documents of upheaval* (edited by Truman Nelson). Hill & Wang, 1969. Paper.
This book consists of selections from Garrison's famous paper, *The Liberator,* published from 1831 to 1865.

(A) Genovese, Eugene D. *Political economy of slavery.* Random, 1965. Paper.
Essays studying the social and economic bases of slavery in the South, and how it drove a deepening wedge into North-South economic development. Marxist bias.

(A) Gilbert, Ben W. *Ten blocks from the White House.* Praeger, 1968. Paper.
Journalistic report on the 1968 Washington race riot. Good for facts, short on analysis. Many illustrations.

(A) Ginzberg, Eli and Alfred S. Eichner. *The troublesome presence: American democracy and the Negro.* Glencoe, 1964. Paper.
History and analysis of the Negro factor in American politics from slavery days to the First World War.

(A) Golden, Harry L. *Mr. Kennedy and the Negroes.* World, 1964.
The noted editor writes about the black struggle for civil rights, with a laudatory point-of-view toward President Kennedy.

(A,Y) Goldston, Robert. *The Negro revolution.* Macmillan, 1968. Paper.
A good overall picture of the history of the Negro from Africa through slavery to the present. It emphasizes the brutal facts rather than glossing over them. Good for secondary school use.

(Y) Goode, Kenneth G. *From Africa to the United States and then ...;
a concise Afro-American history.* Scott, Foresman, 1969.
Paper.

This is exactly what the subtitle says — a concise review of Negro
history in America. Brief sections on specific topics, many lists
of readings, succinct statements of fact — a good book for classroom use. Includes a useful chronological table of events from the
African background to 1968.

(J) Goodman, Walter. *Black bondage: the life of slaves in the South.*
Farrar, 1969.

Description of various phases of slavery; for Junior High School
level. Easy-reading, vivid.

(A,Y) Grant, Joanne (ed.) *Black protest.* Fawcett, 1968. Paper.

Contains a large number of comparatively brief articles, essays
and excerpts of writings on the Negro problem, from slavery days
to the present. Many can be useful for school reference reading.
Good for teachers or students.

(A) Greene, Lorenzo J. *The Negro in colonial New England.* Kennikat,
1942, and Atheneum paperback.

Good account of slave and free Negroes in New England. For
teachers or secondary school research.

(Y) Halasz, Nichols. *The rattling chains.* McKay, 1966.

About Negro unrest and revolt in the South before the Civil War.

(A) Handlin, Oscar. *Race and nationality in American life.* Doubleday,
1957. Paper.

A history of race consciousness in the United States.

(A) Harlan, Louis R. *The Negro in American History.* Amer. Hist.
Assoc., 1965.

A 29-page pamphlet, Publication No. 61, of the Service Center
for Teachers of History.

(Y) Harris, Janet. *Long freedom road; the civil rights story.* McGraw,
1967.

Generally good factual history of the Negro civil rights movement.
Sympathetic but not emotional.

(Y) Harris, Janet and Julius Hobson. *Black pride; a people's struggle.* **McGraw, 1969. Paper.**

A history of the black power movement from slave uprisings to the present. A good synthesis for mature teen-agers, or for adults with little previous background.

(A) Hayden, Tom. *Rebellion in Newark.* **Random, 1967. Paper.**

Account of the race riots in Newark, New Jersey, in July, 1967. Vivid but highly prejudiced against the forces of law.

(A) Haynes, Robert V. (ed.) *Blacks in white America before 1865: issues and interpretations.* **McKay, 1972. Paper.**

Excellent collection of about thirty papers by American scholars, published in recent years, dealing with varied aspects of Negro history. Useful for adult students in the field.

(A) Heacock, Roland. *Understanding the Negro protest.* **Pageant, 1965.**

A good brief analysis of the events that marked the movement for Negro rights between 1954 and 1965. Discusses in clear language the various methods of protest, and includes a chronology of events during the period.

(A) Hersey, John. *The Algiers Motel incident.* **Knopf, 1968. Paper.**

A detailed report of a racial confrontation in the Detroit riots of 1967. Hersey makes the affair an archetype of all the injustices undergone by Negroes in white society.

(A,Y) Higginson, Col. Thomas W. *Army life in a black regiment.* **(edited and abridged by Genevieve S. Gray). Grossett & Dunlap, 1970. Paper.**

Account of the First South Carolina Volunteers, a Union Army battalion of freed slaves commanded by a white officer, Col. Higginson.

(A) Hill, Adelaide and Martin Kilson (comps.) *Apropos of Africa.* **Doubleday, 1971. Paper.**

Large collection of writings and documents dealing with the relationships of American Negroes with Africa throughout our history.

(Y) Hoffman, Edwin D. *Pathways to freedom.* **Houghton, 1964.**

Describes vividly a number of episodes in American history which emphasized human rights. Excellent book for secondary schools.

15

(A) Holland, Jerome H. *Black opportunity.* Weybright & Talley, 1969.
An optimistic analysis of the rise of Negro economic opportunity and buying power; and of the demand in white America for more educated blacks. A book to encourage self-improvement and hope among Negroes.

(A) Hollander, Barnett. *Slavery in America: its legal history.* Barnes & Noble, 1964.
A resource book. It discusses basic legal decisions regarding slavery, from the English common law to the Reconstruction period. Gives extensive quotations from federal and state legislation and court decisions. Useful for historical research.

(A) Holt, Len. *Summer that didn't end.* Morrow, 1965.
First-hand account by a Negro attorney of the events in Mississippi preceding and following the lynching of three civil rights workers.

(A) Hoover, Dwight W. (ed.) *Understanding Negro history.* Quadrangle, 1968. Paper.
Anthology of twenty-four articles, chiefly from scholarly journals. Variety of topics dealing with aspects of Negro history as part of American history. College level reading.

(A) Hornsby, Alton (ed.) *In the cage; eyewitness accounts of the freed Negro in Southern society, 1877-1920.* Quadrangle, 1970.
Good collection of observations and reports by whites, blacks, Americans and Europeans, each of whom was in a position to observe conditions in the South.

(A) Hughes, Langston. *Fight for freedom; the story of the NAACP.* Norton, 1962.
A history of the organization from its founding to the date of publication. Good background material on Negro-American history.

(A,Y) Hughes, Langston and Milton Meltzer. *Pictorial history of the Negro in America.* (rev. ed.) Crown, 1968.
Many types of illustrations on many phases of black history, with textual comment. Especially good for school classrooms or libraries.

(A,Y) Huie, William B. *Three lives for Mississippi.* WCC Books, 1965. Paper.

The story of the 1964 civil rights murders in Mississippi, told by a noted popular writer.

(A) Hyman, Harold M. (ed.) *New frontiers of the American reconstruction.* Univ. of Illinois Press, 1966.

Collection of worthwhile essays on the Reconstruction period, part of which deal with the Negro problem. All follow the "revisionist line."

(A) Ianniello, Lynne (ed.) *Milestones along the march.* Praeger, 1965.

The subtitle describes the book: "12 historic civil rights documents from World War II to Selma."

(J) Jackson, Florence. *The black man in America, 1619-1790.* Watts, 1970.

First of three volumes of Negro history for junior high schools.

(J) Jackson, Florence. *The black man in America, 1791-1861.* Watts, 1971.

Second volume of a text reader for junior high schools, describing the Negro past in the National period. Deals not only with slavery but with the free blacks and some noted leaders. Illustrated. Good library resource.

(J) Jackson, Florence. *The black man in America, 1861-1877.* Watts, 1972.

Third volume in the set previously described. Books are from 80 to 90 pages long, with large print and many illustrations.

(A) Jacobson, Julius (ed.) *The Negro and the American labor movement.* Anchor, 1968.

An historical study.

(A,Y) James, C. L. R. *The black Jacobins: Toussaint L'Ouverture and the San Domingo Revolution.* Random, 1963. 2nd ed. Paper.

Story of a highly successful slave revolt in Haiti. For teachers and high school supplementary reading.

(J) Johnston, Johanna. *Together in America*. Dodd, 1965. **Paper.**
Describes American history as it was affected by the presence of two races, and shows how each made valuable contributions. For school libraries.

(A) Jordan, Winthrop. *White over black*. Univ. of N. Carolina Press, 1968. Penguin, 1969. **Paper.**
Discusses white attitudes toward Negroes in colonial and early national periods. This book is scholarly and received a number of prizes. Holds that racism was an American attitude inherited from England, and that black inferiority was assumed in the earliest settlements.

(A,Y) Katz, William L. *The black West*. Doubleday, 1971.
The story of Negro settlers, cowboys, Indian fighters. Well illustrated. General interest.

(A) Katz, William L. *Eyewitness: the Negro in American history*. Pitman, 1969. **Paper.**
Large and comprehensive book, well-researched and thorough. Combines text, source material and illustrations. Planned for use with secondary school American History courses.

(A,Y) Kay, F. George. *The shameful trade*. Barnes & Co., 1967.
Description of the African slave trade and of slavery, written by an English author. Good general background.

(A) Kellogg, Charles F. *NAACP: A history of the National Association for the Advancement of Colored People*. Johns Hopkins Press, 1967.

(A) King, Martin Luther, Jr. *Stride toward freedom; the Montgomery story*. Harper, 1958. **Paper.**
An account of the 1955 bus boycott in Montgomery, Alabama, which King helped organize.

(A) King, Martin Luther, Jr. *Why we can't wait*. Harper, 1964. **Paper.**
About the crisis in Birmingham, Alabama.

(A) Konvitz, Milton. *A century of civil rights*. Columbia Univ. Press, 1961. Paper.

(A) Kraditor, Aileen S. *Means and ends in American abolitionism*. Pantheon, 1967. Paper.
A scholarly study of Garrison and the debates about abolition in the period 1834-1850. An excellent analysis of the arguments then raging for and against the abolition movement as Garrison personified it. For adult students.

(A) Lader, Lawrence. *The bold Brahmins*. Dutton, 1961.
History of the abolition movement in New England from 1831 to 1863. Well-written and useful for general background, adult or secondary school.

(A) Latham, Frank B. *Rise and fall of "Jim Crow" 1865-1964*. Watts, 1969.
History of the struggle for civil rights.

(Y) Leckie, William H. *Buffalo soldiers*. Univ. of Okla. Press, 1967.
About the use of Negro cavalry in the early days of the West.

(A) Lerner, Gerder (ed.) *Black women in white America: a documentary history*. Pantheon Books, 1972.
Interesting collection of excerpts from books written by Negro women in all periods of American history, giving their viewpoints and experiences.

(A) Lester, Julius. *To be a slave*. Dial, 1968. Paper.
Accounts of slavery by former slaves. Well illustrated.

(Y,J) Levenson, Dorothy. *Reconstruction*. Watts, 1971.
An account for young people of the meaning of the decade after the Civil War.

(A) Levy, Charles J. *Voluntary servitude; whites in the Negro movement*. Appleton, 1968. Paper.

(A) Lewinson, Paul. *Race, class and party.* Russell & Russell, 1959. **Paper.**
The subtitle describes the book's theme: "A history of Negro suffrage and white politics in the South."

(A) Lewis, Anthony. *Portrait of a decade: the second American revolution.* Random, 1964. **Paper.**
A record of the decade 1954-1964 as it relates to civil rights activities. Part of the book consists of excerpts from *New York Times* articles.

(A,Y) Lincoln, C. Eric. *Black Muslims in America.* Beacon, 1961. **Paper.**
Good history of this movement up to 1961. It is objective and well-researched. Suitable for general reading or high school libraries.

(A,Y) Lincoln, C. Eric. *Negro pilgrimage in America.* Praeger, 1969. **Paper.**
A 175-page historical summary of Negro-American history, followed by a chronological list of important events. Useful for public or high school libraries.

(Y) Lindenmeyer, Otto. *Black and brave; the black soldier in America.* McGraw, 1970.
Tells about the part played by Negro soldiers in America's wars. Good for school libraries.

(Y) Liston, Robert. *Slavery in America: the heritage of slavery.* McGraw, 1972.
An account of the failures of black freedom in the years after emancipation.

(A) Litwack, Leon F. *North of slavery; the Negro in the free states, 1790-1860.* Univ. of Chicago Press, 1961. **Paper.**
Study of the position of free blacks in the North, showing that they were strongly discriminated against. Adult students.

(A) Logan, Rayford. *Betrayal of the Negro.* Crowell-Collier, 1965. **Paper.**
A history of Negro injustice from Reconstruction to World War I.

(Y,J) Logan, Rayford and Irving Cohen. *The American Negro: old world background and new world experience.* Houghton, 1967. Paper.

A textbook for junior and senior high schools. A chronological history of the Negro in Africa and America. Rather dull, but full of information. Useful supplement for black studies classes.

(A) Logan, Rayford. *The Negro in the United States. Vol. 1, a history to 1945.* Anvil, 1957. Paper.

Brief summary of American Negro history, with a collection of appropriate documents. Good for teacher use.

(A) Logan, Rayford and Michael Winston. *The Negro in the United States. Vol. 2, the ordeal of democracy.* Van Nostrand, 1972. Paper.

This volume takes up the history of black Americans since 1945. About half the book is text, the remainder contains important documents, mostly legal papers. For senior high school or college classes.

(A) Lomax, Louis E. *The Negro revolt.* Harper, 1962. Paper.

Valuable and interesting study of the Negro militant movement to the date of publication, and especially of the Negro organizations and leaders involved in it.

(A) Lord, Walter. *The past that would not die.* Harper, 1965.

Very readable account of the conflict to get James Meredith admitted to the University of Mississippi, and of the whole background of the issue.

(A) Mabee, Carleton. *Black freedom.* Macmillan, 1970.

Excellent study of the non-violent opponents of slavery before the Civil War, and of the many tactics they used. Has much relevance to today's protest movements. For any library.

(A,Y) Mannix, Daniel and Malcolm Cowley. *Black cargoes: a history of the Atlantic slave trade, 1518-1865.* Viking, 1962. Paper.

Vivid and realistic description of the topic. For teachers and secondary school or public libraries.

(A) Masotti, Louis H. and Jerome Corsi. *Shoot-out in Cleveland*. Praeger, 1969.
A report made for the National Commission on the Causes and Prevention of Violence. Vivid account of the 1968 guerrilla warfare in Cleveland. For any library.

(J) McCarthy, Agnes and Lawrence Reddick. *Worth fighting for*. Doubleday, 1965. Paper.
Negro history for the period of the Civil War and Reconstruction, written for those reading at about the sixth grade level.

(A) McCord, William. *Mississippi: the long hot summer*. Norton, 1965.
The writer, a Stanford University sociologist, here gives an interesting first-hand account of what went on in Mississippi during the summer of 1964.

(A) McKitrick, Eric L. (ed.) *Slavery defended: the views of the Old South*. Prentice, 1963. Paper.
Documents for teacher and student research use.

(Y,J) McPherson, James M. *Marching toward freedom*. Knopf, 1967.
A juvenile account of the part played by Negroes in the Civil War. Objective, with useful and interesting quotations and illustrations.

(A) McPherson, James M. *The Negro's Civil War: how American Negroes felt and acted during the war for Union*. Pantheon, 1965. Paper.
Documentary narrative, scholarly, useful for research reading.

(A) McPherson, James M. *The struggle for equality*. Princeton Univ. Press, 1964. Paper.
Thorough and readable study of abolitionists and Negroes in the Civil War and Reconstruction periods.

(A) Meier, August and Elliott Rudwick. *From plantation to ghetto*. Hill & Wang, 1968. Paper.
Discusses in depth the various Negro protest movements and leaders, chiefly twentieth century. Sound, scholarly, useful to college level students or to teachers.

(A) Meier, August and Elliott Rudwick. *Making of Black America.* Atheneum, 1969. Paper.
Book of nearly a thousand pages, comprised of essays by noted writers on the history of the Negro in America. Very suitable for research and background.

(A) Meier, August. *Negro thought in America: 1880-1915.* Univ. of Michigan Press, 1963. Paper.
A scholarly study for adult students.

(Y) Meltzer, Milton. *Freedom comes to Mississippi.* Follett, 1971.
Story of the post-Civil War reconstruction period, when for a dozen years, blacks had rights.

(A,Y) Meltzer, Milton (ed.) *In their own words; a history of the American Negro.* (Vol. 1, 1619-1865; Vol. 2, 1865-1916; Vol. 3, 1916-1966.) Crowell, 1964-1965. Paper.
Excerpts from important publications by Negroes; speeches, letters, diaries and other sources. Useful for secondary school reference.

(Y) Meltzer, Milton. *Slavery.* Cowles, 1971.
A history of slavery in ancient and medieval Europe.

(Y) Meltzer, Milton and August Meier. *Time of trial, time of hope; the Negro in America, 1919-1945.* Doubleday, 1966. Paper.
A history specifically for teen-agers.

(A) Mendelsohn, Jack. *The martyrs: sixteen who gave their lives for racial justice.* Harper, 1966.
About those who died in the deep South between 1954 and 1964.

(J) Miers, Earl S. *Story of the American Negro.* Wonder Books, 1965.
A very brief (48 pages) summary of the black experience in America for the junior high school level.

(A) Miller, Loren. *The petitioners: the story of the Supreme Court of the U.S. and the Negro.* Pantheon, 1966. Paper.
Written by a Negro judge, this is an authoritative and valuable explanation of the Court's thinking about Negroes from 1789 to 1965.

(A) Mirsky, Jeanette and Allan Nevins. *The world of Eli Whitney.* Macmillan, 1952.
A good study of the cotton industry and slave labor.

(A,Y) Mitchell, J. Paul. *Race riots in black and white.* Prentice, 1970.
An account of various racial disorders from 1863 to 1967 in the United States. Based largely on newspaper sources and written for general reading.

(A) Muse, Benjamin. *American Negro revolution: from non-violence to black power, 1963-67.* Indiana Univ. Press, 1969. Paper.
Detailed description of events and trends in the Negro revolt of those four years.

(A) Muse, Benjamin. *Ten years of prelude; the story of integration since the Supreme Court's 1954 decision.* Viking, 1964.
A scholarly and thorough review of the first ten years' effects of the Brown case.

(A) Myrdal, Gunnar. *An American dilemma.* Harper, 1942, 1962. Paper.
This is a massive work of a thousand pages, with 400 more of notes and appendices. It is the standard study of the Negro in twentieth century America, in all aspects and from all points-of-view. This 20th anniversary edition includes a supplement discussing developments during the two decades since the original publication in 1942.

(A) Nelson, Jack and Jack Bass. *The Orangeburg massacre.* World, 1970.
A journalistic account of a police-student conflict at South Carolina State College at Orangeburg in February, 1968.

(A) Newby, Idus A. *Jim Crow's defense; anti-Negro thought in America, 1900-1930.* Louisiana State Univ. Press, 1965. Paper.
An adult study of white racial prejudice, northern and southern, as expressed in many ways and by many prominent people. Useful in showing the deep roots of racism.

(A) Nichols, Lee. *Breakthrough on the color front.* Random, 1954.
Tells how segregation policies in the armed forces first came to be removed.

(A) Nolen, Claude H. *The Negro's image in the South.* Univ. of Kentucky Press, 1967.

Survey of the sources of anti-Negro prejudice in the South throughout our history.

(A) Nordholt, J. W. Schulte. *The people that walk in darkness* (translated from the original German edition of 1956). Ballantine, 1960. Paper.

A history of the Negro in America. Well-written, for the general public and older youth.

(A) Nye, Russel B. *Fettered freedom.* (Rev. ed.) Mich. State Univ. Press, 1963.

Good historical analysis of the problems of civil liberties, abolitionism and slavery in the period 1830-1860.

(A) Osofsky, Gilbert (ed.) *The burden of race; a documentary history of Negro-white relations in America.* Harper, 1967. Paper.

Good collection in over 600 pages of selected excerpts from many sources on the history of the Negro problem. Court decisions, speeches, articles and other significant exhibits.

(A) Osofsky, Gilbert. *Harlem: the making of a ghetto.* Harper, 1963. Paper.

Interesting history of Harlem from about 1890 to 1920, the period of its basic change from a mixed neighborhood to a black enclave.

(A) Ottley, Roi. *Black odyssey.* John Murray, London, 1949.

Good account of the black experience in America, written by a journalist. Useful in any library.

(A) Ottley, Roi. *No green pastures.* John Murray, London, 1952.

Interesting account of attitudes toward Negroes in a number of European countries, with many of the author's own experiences.

(A) Ovington, Mary W. *The walls came tumbling down.* Harcourt, 1947; Reprinted, Arno Press, 1969. Paper.

An important book of memoirs and Negro rights history by a noted white worker for interracialism in the early part of this century. Good general reading.

(A) Patrick, Rembert W. *The reconstruction of the nation*. Oxford Univ. Press, 1967. Paper.

A scholarly history of the twelve-year post-Civil War period. Excellent for adults wanting an unbiased picture.

(A) Pease, William H. and Jane Pease. *Black Utopia; Negro communal experiments in America*. State Historical Society of Wisconsin, 1963. Paper.

For research and historical background.

(A) Peck, James. *Freedom ride*. Simon & Schuster, 1962.

A short but interesting account of the early civil rights actions in the South. The author was a participant and is, of course, a strong believer in the civil rights cause.

(A,Y) Peeks, Edward. *The long struggle for black power*. Scribner, 1971.

History of Negroes' efforts toward freedom and equal rights. Good for adult or secondary school reading.

(A) Peltason, J. W. *Fifty-eight lonely men; Southern federal judges and school desegregation*. Harcourt, 1961; Univ. of Illinois Press, 1971. Paper.

A study of how the southern federal judges dealt with the 1954 Supreme Court decision. The 1971 edition contains a 1970 epilogue.

(A) Phillips, Ulrich B. *American Negro slavery*. Louisiana Univ. Press, 1966. (2nd rev. ed.) Paper.

Originally written in 1918 by a noted historian with a rather strong pro-Southern bias. Useful for providing an earlier point-of-view.

(A) Pinkney, Alphonso. *Black Americans*. Prentice, 1969. Paper.

A brief historical analysis of the Negro's place in American history. Useful for school or public libraries.

(J) Place, Martin T. *Rifles and war bonnets*. Washburn, 1968.

The story of the two regiments of Negro cavalry who served in the Far West from 1867 to 1891. For upper elementary and lower secondary grades.

(A) Pope-Hennessy, James. *Sins of the fathers*. Knopf, 1968. Paper.
About the African slave traders. A thorough, scholarly, but very interesting account, suitable for any library.

(A,Y) Purdon, Eric. *Black company: the story of subchaser 1264*. McKay, 1972.
Story of the Navy's first all-black crew, written by their commander.

(A) Quarles, Benjamin. *Black abolitionists*. Oxford Univ. Press, 1969. Paper.
Good historical study of the part Negroes played in the abolition movement. Shows that the goals were integration and equality, not separatism.

(A) Quarles, Benjamin. *Lincoln and the Negro*. Oxford Univ. Press, 1962.
A study of Lincoln's attitude, especially in relation to his major concern, winning the war.

(A) Quarles, Benjamin. *The Negro in the American Revolution*. Univ. of N. Carolina Press, 1961. Paper.
An historical study for adult readers.

(A) Quarles, Benjamin. *The Negro in the Civil War*. Russell & Russell, 1953, 1968. Paper.
Good history for general reading.

(A) Quarles, Benjamin. *The Negro in the making of America*. Collier Books, 1964. Paper.
Good general history, especially useful for teachers.

(A) Raper, Arthur F. *The tragedy of lynching*. Dover, 1970.
Originally published in 1933. Report of a 1930 commission that visited the sites of 21 lynchings.

(A) Ratner, Lorman. *Powder keg; Northern opposition to the anti-slavery movement, 1831-1841*. Basic Books, 1968.
A serious and quite readable study for adults interested in American history.

(A) Record, Wilson. *Race and radicalism: the NAACP and the Communist Party in conflict.* Cornell Univ. Press, 1964. Paper.
One of a series of books describing the Communist Party's relationship with various phases of American life and society. This book studies the history of the Party's unsuccessful attempt to drive the Negro rights movement into sedition and communism.

(A) Record, Wilson and Jane Record (eds.) *Little Rock, U.S.A.* Chandler Pub. Co., 1960.
Chronological account of the forced integration of Central High School.

(A) Redding, Saunders. *The lonesome road.* Doubleday, 1958.
An outstanding and very readable history of the Negro people in America, with special attention to some of their more prominent individuals.

(A) Redding, Saunders. *They came in chains.* Lippincott, 1952. Paper.

(A) Redkey, Edwin S. *Black exodus.* Yale Univ. Press, 1970. Paper.
Scholarly study of the various movements in American history looking toward the repatriation of Negroes to Africa.

(A,Y) Reimers, David M. (ed.) *Racism in the United States: an American dilemma?* Holt, 1972. Paper.
Eleven essays on the history and causes of racism. Includes bibliography and other aids for study.

(A) Roche, John P. *Quest for the dream.* Macmillan, 1963.
Very readable, though highly subjective, account of the struggle for civil liberties in the United States since World War I. Covers not only the Negro's rights, but the story of many other oppressed groups. The author is outspokenly liberal.

(A,Y) Rogers, J. A. *Africa's gift to America.* Futoro, 1961.
Good and unusual illustrations about the Negro in early America make this useful in classrooms or as a teacher source.

(A) Rose, Arnold. *The Negro in America.* Beacon, 1964. Paper.
This is a condensation of Myrdal's classic, *An American Dilemma.*

(A) Rose, Arnold M. (ed.) *Assuring freedom to the free; a century of emancipation in the United States.* Wayne State Univ. Press, 1964.
Collection of twelve papers presented as lectures at Wayne State in 1963 by as many specialists. Covers a variety of Negro problems as they developed over a century.

(A) Rose, Peter (ed.) *Americans from Africa.* 2 vols. Atherton, 1969. Paper.
Very comprehensive collection of essays on many aspects of black history. Good basic source material for any general library.

(A) Rose, Willie Lee. *Rehearsal for reconstruction: the Port Royal experiment.* Random, 1967. Paper.
Tells the story of the ten thousand slaves of the Sea Islands off South Carolina who became the first freedmen in 1861.

(A) Rudwick, Elliott M. *Race riot at East St. Louis, July 2, 1917.* Southern Illinois Univ. Press, 1964.
Detailed account and analysis of the event, with data seeking to find similarities between it and more recent riots.

(A) St. James, Warren D. *The National Association for the Advancement of Colored People.* Exposition Press, 1958.
A history of the organization from its founding to publication date.

(A) Saunders, Doris E. *The day they marched.* Johnson Pub. Co., 1963. Paper.
An account of the 1963 civil rights march in Washington.

(A) Sauter, Van Gordon and Burleigh Hines. *Nightmare in Detroit.* Regnery, 1968.
The authors are newspapermen reporting in detail on the 1967 race riot in Detroit. Vivid and interesting reading.

(A) Scheiner, Seth M. *Negro Mecca: a history of the Negro in New York City, 1865-1920.* New York Univ. Press, 1965. Paper.
A study of how and why Harlem became a black community.

(A) Scheiner, Seth M. and Tilden Edelstein (eds.) *The black Americans: interpretive readings.* Holt, 1971. Paper.
A 500-page anthology of essays on the history of the American Negro. Valuable background material.

(A) Segal, Ronald. *The race war.* Viking, 1967. Paper.
A serious and scholarly book, good for background information on the whole problem of race conflict throughout the world. It gives the history of racism not only in the United States, but in Africa, England, Russia, China and elsewhere.

(A) Shade, William G. and Roy C. Herrenkohl. *Seven on black.* Lippincott, 1970. Paper.
Seven essays based on a series of college lectures dealing with a variety of topics in black history in America. Good background material for black studies courses.

(A) Shapiro, Fred and James Sullivan. *Race riot, New York, 1964.* Crowell, 1964.
Two reporters give a first-hand picture in detail of the riots in New York City in July, 1964.

(A) Shogan, Robert. *The Detroit race riot; a study in violence.* Chilton, 1964.
Detailed and objective account of the 1943 occurrence.

(A) Singletary, Otis. *The South in American history.* Amer. Hist. Assoc., 1957.
One of the publications of the Service Center for Teachers in History.

(A) Sochen, June (ed.) *The black man and the American dream 1900-1930; Negro aspirations in America.* Quadrangle, 1971.
Anthology of articles written by black authors chiefly directed at white readers of popular magazines of the indicated period.

(Y,J) Spangler, Earl. *The Negro in America.* Lerner, 1966.
A reader for use in middle grades.

(A) Spear, Allan. *Black Chicago: the making of a Negro ghetto, 1890-1920.* Univ. of Chicago Press, 1969. Paper.
First historical study of the Negro slums of Chicago, which have been the subject of many novels. Explains how ghettos developed.

(A) Stampp, Kenneth M. *Era of reconstruction, 1865-1877.* Knopf, 1965. Paper.
A study of political conditions, including black roles.

(A) Stampp, Kenneth M. *The peculiar institution.* Random, 1956. Paper.
Thorough study of slavery in American history — an outstanding work.

(A,Y) Starkey, Marion L. *Striving to make it my home.* Norton, 1964.
The story of the slave trade and early slavery. Good reading for secondary schools.

(A) Staudenraus, P. J. *The African colonization movement, 1816-1865.* Columbia Univ. Press, 1961.
Scholarly history of the pre-Civil War efforts to return Negroes to Africa. For serious students of history.

(J) Sterling, Dorothy. *Forever free.* Doubleday, 1963.
Story of the Emancipation Proclamation and of slavery prior to it. Well-written and authentic.

(Y,J) Sterling, Dorothy. *Tear down the walls!* Doubleday, 1968. Paper.
A history of Negroes in the United States and of the civil rights movement and its various organizations. Well and interestingly written to make the story real for juveniles.

(A) Sternsher, Bernard (ed.) *The Negro in depression and war; prelude to revolution, 1930-1945.* Quadrangle, 1969. Paper.
Writings by black and white authors on the actions and relationships between the F.D.R. administration and the black population.

(Y) Stevenson, Janet. *The Montgomery bus boycott.* Watts, 1971.
A brief but good account of this famous 1955 civil rights action; for grades 7-12.

(A,Y) Sutherland, Elizabeth (ed.) *Letters from Mississippi.* McGraw, 1965.
Well-edited selections from letters written home in the summer of 1964 by the white students who went South to work for civil rights. Valuable first-hand picture for students and general readers.

(J) Swift, Hildegarde. *North star shining.* Morrow, 1947.
For elementary pupils, a pictorial history of the American Negro.

(A) Synnestvedt, Sig. *The white response to black emancipation.* Macmillan, 1972.
A study of how white Americans and their institutions have resisted the black effort for equal rights.

(A) Tannenbaum, Frank. *Slave and citizen.* Random, 1963. Paper.
Comparison of slavery in the United States with its counterpart in Latin America.

(Y) Thorp, Earl E. (ed.) *Black experience in America.* American Education Publications, 1971. Paper.
A series of six 48-page pamphlets, each prepared by a different author, for secondary or junior school classroom use. They deal with the period from Reconstruction to the present. Each pamphlet, with numerous illustrations, tells about the Negro experience at a particular period. They are simply told for students, and there is a brief teacher's guide. Very useful for a survey of race history.

(A) Tindall, George A. *South Carolina Negroes, 1877-1900.* Univ. of South Carolina Press, 1952. Paper.
A detailed and researched picture of the life and condition of the Southern Negro.

(A) Toplin, Robert B. *The abolition of slavery in Brazil.* Atheneum, 1972.
For any reader interested in racial or Latin-American history, this is a scholarly account of the growth and final success, in 1888, of the abolition movement in Brazil.

(A) Tuttle, William M., Jr. *Race riot; Chicago in the red summer of 1919.* **Atheneum, 1970.**
Thorough account of the riot which saw thirty-eight persons killed, and an analysis of conditions which led to it. Well researched, good general reading.

(A) Twombly, Robert C. (ed.) *Blacks in white America since 1865.* **McKay, 1971.**
An anthology of thirty-seven excerpts from writers both black and white, dealing with race questions. All are strongly pro-Negro. Introductory sections by the editor.

(A) Vincent, Theodore. *Black power and the Garvey movement.* **Ramparts, 1971.**
Scholarly adult study of Marcus Garvey's black nationalist movement of the 1920's.

(A) Voegeli, V. J. *Free but not equal.* **Univ. of Chicago Press, 1967. Paper.**
Scholarly study of racialism and anti-Negro feeling in the Middle West during the Civil War, and how these affected governmental decisions.

(A) Von Hoffman, Nicholas. *Mississippi notebook.* **White, 1964.**
The author was a Chicago reporter who covered the civil rights uprisings in Mississippi in 1964. The book, with many excellent photographs, is an interesting account of what he saw.

(A) Wade, Richard C. *Slavery in the cities: the South 1820-1860.* **Oxford Univ. Press, 1964. Paper.**
Studies the nature of slavery in Southern cities, and shows that it tended to die out, partly because of the dangers inherent in making slaves more experienced and sophisticated.

(A) Walvin, James. *The black presence.* **Schocken Books, 1972.**
A history of the Negro in England from 1555 to 1860. Consists of extensive analysis and accompanying documents.

(A) Warren, Robert Penn. *Segregation; the inner conflict in the South.* **Random, 1956. Paper.**
Brief interesting report on the author's return to the South to interview a number of people about the impact of integration.

(A) Warren, Robert Penn. *Who speaks for the Negro?* Random, 1965. Paper.

The popular novelist here has provided a fascinating collection of conversations with Negroes north and south about the race problem as they see it. All the discussions are from taped interviews, skillfully described and connected by Mr. Warren.

(A) Waskow, Arthur. *From race riot to sit-in, 1919 and the 1960's.* Doubleday, 1966. Paper.

A scholarly analysis and comparison of racial violence in these two periods.

(A) Watters, Pat and Reese Cleghorn. *Climbing Jacob's ladder; the arrival of Negroes in Southern politics.* Harcourt, 1967. Paper.

An account of the Negro struggle for the vote in the South in the 1960's. Good background for the adult reader seeking definitive information.

(A) Weinstein, Allen and Frank Gatell (eds.) *American Negro slavery: a modern reader.* Oxford Univ. Press, 1968. Paper.

A good collection, with bibliography, of twenty-two essays on slavery.

(A) Weinstein, Allen and Frank Gatell (eds.) *The segregation era, 1863-1954.* Oxford Univ. Press, 1970. Paper.

Nineteen essays dealing with Negro history in this period. Useful background for black studies courses.

(A) Werstein, Irving. *A proud people: black Americans.* Lippincott, 1970.

General history of the Negro in America.

(A) Wesley, Charles and Patricia Romero. *Negro Americans in the Civil War.* United Publishers Co., 1967.

(A) Weyl, Nathaniel and William Marina. *American statesmen on slavery and the Negro.* Arlington House, 1971.

A well-written study of the attitudes of many noted Americans over two centuries on the race question, showing that many of our most respected leaders were prejudiced.

(A) Wharton, Vernon L. *The Negro in Mississippi 1865-1890.* Harper, 1947. Paper.
A scholarly study of the black position during and after Reconstruction.

(A) Williamson, Joel. *After slavery.* Univ. of North Carolina Press, 1965. Paper.
A study of the Reconstruction years in South Carolina. Shows that the freedmen made a good deal of progress until the return of Democratic Party control.

(A,Y) Wilson, Elinor. *Jim Beckwourth.* Univ. of Okla. Press, 1972.
A eulogistic biography of a black frontiersman almost unknown until the recent revival of black heroes in history.

(A) Wilson, Joseph T. *The black phalanx.* Arno, 1968.
First published in 1890, this is a history of Negro participation in the Revolution, War of 1812 and Civil War, written by a black man who served through the latter and became an officer in the G.A.R.

(A) Wilson, Theodore B. *The black codes of the South.* Univ. of Alabama Press, 1965.
The only book that deals solely with these Negro control laws of 1865-66 and their motivation. Primarily for specialists in the period.

(A) Winks, Robin W. *The blacks in Canada.* Yale Univ. Press, 1970.
Serious and very thorough study of black history in Canada and the problems that have developed there.

(A) Wish, Harvey (ed.) *Slavery in the South.* Farrar, 1964. Paper.
Sixteen items representing writings by former slaves, Northern and British authors, and Southern whites. Good picture of slavery from a number of viewpoints.

(A) Wolff, Miles. *Lunch at the five and ten.* Stein & Day, 1970.
Interesting account of the Negro sit-in action of 1960, beginning with the sit-in by four young people at the Woolworth lunch counter in Greensboro, North Carolina.

(J) Woodin, G. Bruce. *Slavery (1850-1877).* Sterling Pub. Co., 1972.
A 90-page history written for grades 4-6. The type is large and it is well illustrated. The book is volume four of a series called "A Fresh Look at American History."

(A) Woodson, Carter G. *A century of Negro migration.* Russell & Russell, 1918, 1969.
History of the northward movement of Negroes up to 1918.

(Y) Woodson, Carter G. *Story of the Negro retold.* Assoc. Publishers, 1959. Paper.
Revised edition of an original 1935 book prepared for secondary schools.

(A) Woodson, Carter G. and Charles Wesley. *The Negro in our history.* Assoc. Publishers, 1966 (11th ed.)
Originally published by Woodson in 1922, and here updated by Wesley, in its 11th edition. An 800-page history, comprehensive and interesting, especially for the point-of-view of fifty years ago. The revision has been only in adding a number of chapters on more recent developments.

(A) Woodward, C. Vann. *Origins of the New South.* Louisiana State Univ. Press, 1951. Paper.
Perhaps the standard work on the South since the Civil War.

(A) Woodward, C. Vann. *Strange career of Jim Crow.* Oxford Univ. Press, 1966. (2nd ed.) Paper.
Holds that the roots of segregation were in the 1890's and actually developed mostly in the North.

(A) Wynes, Charles E. (ed.) *Negro in the South since 1865.* Univ. of Alabama Press, 1965. Paper.
Eleven essays by as many current historians, taken from scholarly journals. They deal with various phases of the Negro's place in the South.

(A) Zilversmit, Arthur. *The first emancipation.* Univ. of Chicago Press, 1967. Paper.
Doctoral dissertation studying the history of emancipation of Negroes in the North, and of the role of free Negro labor there.

(A) Zinn, Howard. *SNCC: the new abolitionists.* Beacon, 1964. Paper.
Interesting story of the origin and activities of this group, by a college professor who was one of its advisors.

PART II

BIOGRAPHY, MEMOIRS, AUTOBIOGRAPHY

(A,Y) Adams, John R. *Harriet Beecher Stowe.* Twayne, 1964. Paper.
A biography for adults or secondary school students.

(A,Y) Adams, Russell L. *Great Negroes, past and present.* Afro-American Pub. Co., 1963. Paper.
Good collection of some 160 brief biographical sketches, about a page each, very suitable for school libraries. The great majority of subjects are Negro Americans, though there are some sketches of modern African leaders. Good readable style, and portraits of each person.

(Y) Alexander, Ray Pace (ed.) *Young and black in America.* Random, 1970.
This is a good anthology of moving excerpts from eight black autobiographies, including Douglass, Wright, Edwards and others.

(A,Y) Anderson, Margaret. *The children of the South.* Farrar, 1966. Paper.
First published in 1958, this is a very useful and readable book by a teacher in Clinton, Tennesseee, who witnessed some of the most violent reactions to the 1954 Supreme Court decision. The author's approach is a very human one. Good for high school pupils.

(Y) Angell, Pauline. *To the top of the world.* Rand McNally, 1964.
The lives of Peary and his Negro companion, Henson. For secondary schools.

(A,Y) Angelou, Maya. *I know why the caged bird sings.* Random, 1970. Paper.
A black woman's memoirs of her youth. Good supplementary reading.

(Y) Ansley, Delight. *Sword and the spirit; a life of John Brown.* Crowell, 1955.
Well-written biography for teen-agers.

(A) Bardolph, Richard. *Negro vanguard.* Random, 1959. Paper.
A 500-page collective biography, or series of biographical sketches, of several hundred Negroes who became prominent during the past two centuries. They are described as members of groups — artists, educators, athletes, etc. — in various periods of time. Includes good bibliographical material.

(Y) Bartlett, Irving H. *Wendell Phillips; Brahmin radical.* Beacon, 1961.
Biography for young people.

(A,Y) Bates, Daisy. *The long shadow of Little Rock: a memoir.* McKay, 1962.
Mrs. Bates led the fight to get the Negro children into Central High School. This is her story of the affair, vivid and highly subjective.

(A) Beam, Lura. *He called them by the lightning.* Bobbs, 1967.
Interesting and well-written memoir by a white woman who taught in the Negro schools of the South from 1908 to 1919. Her recollections make this a valuable picture of one phase of Negro American history, and of Southern style of life at that time.

(A) Bedini, Silvio. *The life of Benjamin Banneker.* Scribner, 1971.
Biography of an outstanding 18th century Negro. For general reading.

(A,Y) Belfrage, Sally. *Freedom summer.* Viking, 1965. Paper.
The author, a white girl from the North, was one of the volunteer civil rights workers in Mississippi in the summer of 1964. This is her very interesting account of her experiences.

(A,Y) Bennett, Lerone, Jr. *Pioneers in protest.* Johnson Pub. Co., 1968. Paper.
Biographical sketches of about fifteen pages each of twenty men and women of both races who were prominent in the Negro cause. Interestingly written, and good for high school supplementary reading.

(Y) Bennett, Lerone, Jr. *What manner of man!* Johnson Pub. Co., 1965. Paper.
Biography of Marin Luther King, Jr.

(Y) Bernard, Jacqueline. *Journey toward freedom; the story of Sojourner Truth.* Norton, 1967. Paper.
Good biography for young people of a noted black fighter for freedom and equality.

(A) Bleiweiss, Robert M. (ed.) *Marching to freedom; the life of Martin Luther King, Jr.* Amer. Education Publications, 1968.

(Y,J) Bontemps, Arna. *Famous Negro athletes.* Dodd, 1964. Paper.
Short biographies, interesting and favorable. Especially suitable for secondary school level.

(Y,J) Bontemps, Arna. *Frederick Douglass: slave, fighter, freeman.* Knopf, 1959.

(A) Bontemps, Arna. *Free at last.* Dodd, 1971.
Biography of Frederick Douglass.

(A,Y) Bontemps, Arna (ed.) *Great slave narratives.* Beacon, 1969. Paper.
A collection of accounts of what slavery was like, written by people who had lived in slavery and escaped from it. Good original source material for adults or teen-agers.

(Y) Bontemps, Arna. *100 years of Negro freedom.* Dodd, 1967. Paper.
The stories of Negro leaders in American history during the period since the Civil War. Useful supplementary high school material.

(Y) Bontemps, Arna. *We have tomorrow.* Houghton, 1945.
Short biographies of twelve contemporary Negroes who in various ways overcame racial handicaps to become successful in some line of achievement.

(A,Y) Bontemps, Arna and Jack Conroy. *Anyplace but here.* Hill & Wang, 1966.
About Du Sable, Beckwourth and other Negro pathfinders, as well as many interesting figures in black history.

(A) Boyle, Sarah. *The desegregated heart.* Morrow, 1962. Paper.
An interesting account of a white Southern woman's efforts to fight segregation in Viriginia in the early 1960's.

(A,Y) Braden, Anne. *The wall between.* Monthly Review Press, 1958.
Personal account of racial violence in Louisville in 1954, told by a white family who triggered it by selling a home to a Negro. Good for high school or general library.

(A) Bradford, Perry. *Born with the blues.* Oak, 1965. Paper.
Memoirs and autobiography of a Negro jazz musician. Many photographs of old-time notables in this field.

(Y) Bradford, Sarah. *Harriet Tubman, Moses of her people.* Peter Smith, 1961. Paper.

(A) Breitman, George. *The last year of Malcolm X; the evolution of a revolutionary.* Merit, 1967. Paper.
A study of this leader's rise to importance. Undergraduate college and adult level.

(A) Broderick, Francis L. *W. E. B. DuBois, Negro leader in a time of crisis.* Stanford Univ. Press, 1959. Paper.
One of the better biographies of this noted black leader.

(A,Y) Brown, Claude. *Manchild in the promised land.* Macmillan, 1965. Paper.
Highly readable autobiography of a black man's experiences growing up in Harlem, and how he made his way out of it.

(Y) Bruner, Richard W. *Whitney M. Young, Jr.* McKay, 1972.
Book for young adults about this highly respected leader.

(A) Canzoneri, Robert. *"I do so politely"; a voice from the South.* Houghton, 1965.
Reminiscences, and considerations about Southern attitudes, by a young native of Mississippi of Italian descent, now living in California. Brief, well-written, anti-racist.

(J) Carruth, Ella. *She wanted to read.* Abingdon, 1966. Paper.
A biography for elementary schools of Mary McLeod Bethune.

(J) Chernow, Fred and Carol. *Reading exercises in Negro history.* Continental Press, 1968.
Short biographical sketches for about fourth grade level.

(A) Christopher, Maurine. *America's black Congressmen.* Crowell, 1971.
Biographical sketches of the thirty-four Negroes who have served in Congress up to 1970.

(A) Clark, Septima. *Echo in my soul.* Dutton, 1962.
A dedicated colored teacher describes her long career in the school systems of the South, and her later work with the Citizenship Schools of the Southern Christian Leadership Conference. A warm and human memoir.

(Y) Clayton, Edward T. *Martin Luther King, Jr.; the peaceful warrior.* Prentice, 1964. Paper.
Brief, simple, very readable biography for secondary school use.

(A) Cleaver, Eldridge. *Soul on ice.* McGraw, 1967.
Collection of essays and letters by this leading black militant, explaining his theories about the black man's destiny.

(Y) Cole, Hubert. *Christophe: King of Haiti.* Viking, 1967. Paper.
History of the French colony and the revolution there. Secondary school reading.

(A) Coles, Robert. *Children of crisis: a study of courage and fear*. **Little, 1967. Paper.**
Written by a physician, a child specialist, working in the South. He studies here the effects of racism and school conditions on children, using many case studies. Good adult background material, especially on the school desegregation problem.

(A) Cornwall, Barbara. *The bush rebels; a personal account of black revolt in Africa*. **Holt, 1972.**
First-hand report by an American journalist of her experiences with the rebels struggling against Portuguese rule in Mozambique and Guinea.

(Y) Cortesi, Lawrence. *Jim Beckwourth*. **Criterion, 1970.**
Life of the noted Negro explorer and western frontiersman.

(A) Creger, Ralph. *A look down the lonesome road*. **Doubleday, 1964.**
Very readable personal recollections of a white liberal in the South and his experiences with segregationists. For the general reader and any library.

(A,Y) Cronon, Edmund. *Black Moses; the story of Marcus Garvey*. **Univ. of Wisconsin, 1955. Paper.**
Biography of Marcus Garvey, promoter of black nationalism.

(A) Cutler, John H. *Ed Brooke; a biography of a Senator*. **Bobbs, 1972.**
A 400-page account of the first black U.S. Senator since the days of Reconstruction.

(A,Y) David, Jay (ed.) *Growing up black*. **Morrow, 1968. Paper.**
Nineteen excerpts from the autobiographies of as many Negro Americans, from Booker T. Washington to Dick Gregory. The excerpts are the childhood experiences of the writers. Good material for high school reading.

(Y,J) David, Jay and Catherine Greene (eds.) *Black roots*. **Lothrop, 1971.**
Excerpts about childhood from the autobiographies of twenty black Americans, each introduced by a biographical sketch. Good reading for middle and secondary schools.

(A,Y) David, Jay and Elaine Crane (eds.) *The black soldier.* Morrow, 1971.

Excerpts from many sources all dealing with the sad picture of Negro soldiers from the Revolution to Vietnam whose status was always second-class.

(A,Y) Davis, Daniel S. *Marcus Garvey.* Watts, 1972.

A biography, suitable for high schools, of the flamboyant black leader who in the 1920's was best known for his program for resettling American Negroes in an independent African state. Illustrated.

(A,Y) Decker, Sunny. *An empty spoon.* Harper, 1969. Paper.

The author was a well-educated young woman from Main Line Philadelphia who chose to teach English in a black high school. She tells of her experiences, and of her finding that identifying with the ghetto children came ahead of teaching literature.

(J) Dobler, Lavinia and Edgar Toppin. *Pioneers and patriots.* Doubleday, 1965. Paper.

The stories of six colonial and Revolutionary Negroes who were important in various ways. Illustrated.

(Y) Douglass, Frederick. *Life and times* (as abridged by Barbara Ritchie). Thos. Y. Crowell, 1966.

An abridgement of Douglass' autobiography, very suitable for junior or senior high schools.

(Y) Douglass, Frederick. *Narrative of the life of Frederick Douglass, an American slave.* Doubleday, 1963. Paper.

This is a reprint of the original of 1845, one of three autobiographical narratives by Douglass. Suitable for secondary school reading.

(Y,J) Douty, Esther. *Forten, the sailmaker; pioneer champion of Negro rights.* Rand McNally, 1968.

Good biography suitable for secondary school use.

(A,Y) Drotning, Phillip T. *Black heroes in our nation's history.* Cowles, 1969. Paper.

Collection of short biographical sketches of Negroes, some well-known, others not. Good bibliography.

(A,Y) Drotning, Phillip T. and Wesley W. South. *Up from the ghetto.*
Cowles, 1970. Paper.
Fourteen stories of blacks who have made it from slums to success.
Good for school supplementary reading.

(A,Y) DuBois, Shirley G. *His day is marching on: a memoir of W. E. B.
DuBois.* Lippincott, 1971.
An excellent study of DuBois, written by his wife. Good supplementary reading, especially in conjunction with DuBois' autobiography.

(A) DuBois, W. E. B. *Autobiography.* International Publishers Co., 1968.
Paper.
Subjective but valuable for teachers and older students.

(A) DuBois, W. E. B. *The gift of black folk.* Afro-Amer. Pub. Co., 1969.
Paper.
About a number of outstanding Negroes in American culture.
Originally published in 1924.

(A) Edmonds, Helen G. *Black faces in high places.* Harcourt, 1971.
This is an historical account of the impact of Negroes on government offices in the last decade or two. It covers all levels and the
three branches, giving identifying information about many individuals. Good library resource.

(A) Ehle, John. *The freemen.* Harper, 1965.
A first-person account and analysis of the civil rights disorders in
Chapel Hill, North Carolina, in 1963-64.

(Y) Fax, Elton C. *Contemporary black leaders.* Dodd, 1970.
Fourteen biographical sketches, interestingly written for secondary
school level. Good for reading or reference.

(A) Fax, Elton C. *Garvey, the story of a pioneer black nationalist.* Dodd,
1972.
Very readable biography of Marcus Garvey and history of his
times.

(Y,J) Felton, Harold. *Edward Rose, Negro trail blazer.* Dodd, 1967.
The story of an early Negro trapper and frontiersman, written for junior high school level.

(J) Felton, Harold. *Jim Beckwourth, Negro mountain man.* Dodd, 1966. Paper.
Biography for the junior high level.

(J) Felton, Harold. *Nat Love, Negro cowboy.* Dodd, 1969.
Illustrated biography for junior high level.

(J) Fenderson, Lewis H. *Daniel Hale Williams, open heart doctor.* McGraw, 1972.
Biography of an important Negro surgeon. Junior high grades.

(Y,J) Fenderson, Lewis H. *Thurgood Marshall, fighter for justice.* McGraw, 1969.

(A) Ferguson, Blanche. *Countee Cullen and the Negro Renaissance.* Dodd, 1966. Paper.
One of the few works dealing in some detail with the life of an important Negro poet of the late 1920's.

(Y) Flynn, James J. *Negroes of achievement in modern America.* Dodd, 1970.
Collection of 22 brief biographical sketches of noted Negroes of the past few years. Good supplementary reading material.

(A) Foner, Eric (ed.) *Nat Turner.* Prentice, 1971.
Analysis, contemporary comments and modern research.

(A) Fox, Stephen R. *The guardian of Boston, William Monroe Trotter.* Atheneum, 1969. Paper.
Biography of the founder of the *Boston Guardian* and an important twentieth century black leader.

(A) Frederickson, George (ed.) *William Lloyd Garrison.* Prentice, 1968. Paper.
Excerpts from his papers, contrasting evaluations by his contemporaries, and by historians.

(A) Garvey, Amy J. *Garvey and Garveyism.* Collier Macmillan Co., 1963. Paper.
Garvey's wife writes about the Universal Negro Improvement Association and its after-effects.

(Y) Gatheru, Rueul. *Child of two worlds: a Kikuyu's story.* Doubleday, 1966. Paper.
Autobiography of a young Kenyan who grew up in East Africa and was in the United States during the Mau Mau war. Good supplementary high school reading.

(Y) Gorham, Charles O. *Lion of Judah: a life of Haile Selassie.* Farrar, 1966.
Well-written, interesting reading.

(Y,J) Graham, Shirley. *Booker T. Washington.* Messner, 1966.
Rather fictionalized biography — junior and senior high school level.

(Y,J) Graham, Shirley. *Jean Baptiste Pointe du Sable.* Messner, 1953.
Fictionalized biography of the Negro who was Chicago's first settler.

(J) Graham, Shirley. *Story of Paul Robeson.* Messner, 1967.
A good biography, recommended for intermediate grades.

(J) Graham, Shirley. *Story of Phyllis Wheatley.* Messner, 1949. Paper.
About the colonial Negro poetess who gained international fame.

(Y) Graham, Shirley. *There was once a slave.* Messner, 1947.
Well-written biography of Frederick Douglass.

(J) Graham, Shirley. *Your most humble servant.* Messner, 1949.
About Benjamin Banneker, Negro scientist and planner, who helped lay out Washington, D. C. For intermediate grades.

(Y) Gray, Genevieve S. (ed.) *Life and times of Frederick Douglass.* Grosset & Dunlop, 1970.
A modernized abridgement of Douglass' autobiography. Suitable for secondary school use.

(Y) Gregory, Susan. *Hey, white girl!* Norton, 1970. Paper.
The diary of a white girl who spent a year as the only white student in a Negro ghetto high school in Chicago. Her family was deeply committed to working against slum conditions. The book is mature and very perceptive of the problems.

(Y,J) Haber, Louis. *Black pioneers of science and invention.* Harcourt, 1970.
Seven biographical sketches, good for school supplementary reading.

(J) Halliburton, Warren. *The picture life of Jesse Jackson.* Watts, 1972.
The Rev. Jesse Jackson is a noted black leader in Chicago. This is a short biography for lower elementary schools, with large print and photographs.

(A) Halsell, Grace. *Soul sister.* World, 1968. Paper.
A white Texas woman reporter darkened her skin and worked in Harlem for six months as a Negro. This is a report on what she saw. Interesting for the general reader.

(A) Harkey, Ira B. *Smell of burning crosses.* Harris-Wolfe, 1967.
Fascinating story by a noted Mississippi newspaper editor of his fight against bigotry. For school or public libraries.

(A) Harlan, Louis R. *Booker T. Washington; the making of a black leader, 1856-1901.* Oxford Univ. Press, 1972.
A serious, full-length biography, but well-written and very readable.

(A) Harris, Sheldon H. *Paul Cuffe.* **Simon & Schuster, 1972. Paper.**
The biography of a mixed-race New England ship-owner who repatriated thirty-eight blacks to West Africa in 1815. He was one of the first to have the vision of this solution to the slave problem.

(A) Haskins, James. *Diary of a Harlem schoolteacher.* **Grove, 1969. Paper.**
Highly interesting but deeply depressing picture of "education" at about its worst. May be read as an antidote to over-idealistic pedagogical manuals.

(A) Haskins, James. *A piece of the power: four black mayors.* **Dial, 1972.**
A study, partly biographical, of Stokes, Hatcher, Evers and Gibson, and the significance of their election to office.

(A,Y) Haskins, James. *Profiles in black power.* **Doubleday, 1970.**
Eleven black leaders are analyzed for their influence on the black power movement.

(A) Hawkins, Hugh (ed.) *Booker T. Washington and his critics: the problem of Negro leadership.* **Heath, 1962. Paper.**

(Y) Heard, J. Norman. *The black frontiersmen.* **Day, 1970.**
The stories of the Negroes who played parts in the opening of the West. Good supplementary high school reading.

(A) Hedgeman, Anna. *The trumpet sounds.* **Holt, 1964.**
A notable Negro leader tells of her wide and varied experience in working for Negro betterment, and of the gains made in civil rights.

(Y) Henson, Matthew. *A black explorer at the North Pole.* **Walker, 1969.**
Originally published in 1912, this is the journal of the Negro who accompanied Peary to the Pole in 1909.

(A) Herndon, James. *The way it spozed to be.* Simon & Schuster, 1968. Paper.

The writer reports on a year spent trying to teach in a black ghetto school in California.

(J) Herschler, Mildred. *Frederick Douglass.* Follett, 1969.

Very readable biography for upper elementary grades.

(Y) Hoexter, Corinne K. *Black crusader: Frederick Douglass.* Rand McNally, 1970.

A biography for teen-agers.

(A,Y) Holt, Margaret V. *George Washington Carver.* Doubleday, 1963.

(A,Y) Holt, Rackham. *Mary McLeod Bethune; a biography.* Doubleday, 1964.

Suitable for reading at secondary or adult level, this is the story of a noted Negro woman educator.

(A,Y) Hoyt, Edwin P. *Paul Robeson, the American Othello.* World, 1967.

(Y,J) Hughes, Langston. *Famous Negro heroes of America.* Dodd, 1958.

Contains sixteen biographical stories, well-written for young people.

(Y,J) Hughes, Langston. *Famous Negro music-makers.* Dodd, 1955.

Collection of short biographical sketches especially for young people.

(J) Humphreville, Frances. *Harriet Tubman; flame of freedom.* Houghton, 1967.

A biography for elementary pupils.

(A) Jackson, George. *Soledad brother.* **Coward, 1970. Paper.**
Jackson, who was a black convict in Soledad Prison in California wrote these letters to his family and friends, explaining his rage at racial injustice, and his determination not to be beaten down by prison routine. A powerful book of self-revelation.

(A) Johnson, James Weldon. *Along this way.* **Viking, 1933. Paper.**
The autobiography of a noted Negro. Good general reading.

(J) Johnston, Johanna. *A special bravery.* **Dodd, 1967. Paper.**
Sketches of fifteen American Negroes, from Crispus Attucks to Dr. King.

(A,Y) Johnston, Johanna. *Runaway to heaven: the story of Harriet Beecher Stowe.* **Doubleday, 1963.**

(A) Kendall, Robert. *White teacher in a black school.* **Devin-Adair, 1964.**
Personal experiences of a young white man who attempted for two years to teach English in a black school in Los Angeles. He found it impossible to do, and chiefly blamed school administrators for doing nothing about it.

(Y) Kennerly, Karen (ed.) *The slave who bought his freedom.* **Dutton, 1971.**
Adaptation of an autobiography written in 1789 by a former slave, brought from Africa as a child, and who later gained his freedom.

(Y,J) Killens, John O. *Great gittin' up morning.* **Doubleday, 1972.**
Partly fictionalized biography of a slave who became a leader of his people in Charleston, S. C., and helped to form a conspiracy against the whites. Middle school level.

(Y,J) King, John T. and Marcet. *Famous Negro Americans.* **Steck-Vaughn Co., 1967. Paper.**
Short easy-to-read biographical sketches of twenty-three noted Negroes, past and contemporary.

50

(Y) Knight, Michael (ed.) *In chains to Louisiana.* **Dutton, 1971.**
The autobiographical account of a Negro, born free in New York, who was kidnaped in Washington in 1841 and who spent twelve years in slavery in Louisiana.

(A) Kohl, Herbert R. *36 children.* **New American Library, 1967. Paper.**
Excellent account of the author's experiences teaching a sixth grade in Harlem. Much of the book reproduces student efforts and growth.

(A) Korngold, Ralph. *Citizen Toussaint.* **Little, 1944. Paper.**
A biography of Toussaint L'Ouverture.

(A) Korngold, Ralph. *Thaddeus Stevens.* **Harcourt, 1955.**
A sympathetic portrait of a very misunderstood figure of the Civil War era.

(A) Kozol, Jonathan. *Death at an early age.* **Houghton, 1967. Paper.**
The subtitle is "The destruction of the hearts and minds of Negro children in the Boston public schools," and the book gives a highly critical and subjective picture of a fourth grade teaching experience.

(Y) Kugelmass, J. Alvin. *Ralph J. Bunche; fighter for peace.* **Messner, 1952.**
A biography for young people.; Although out-dated, it is still useful.

(A) Kunstler, William M. *Deep in my heart.* **Morrow, 1966. Paper.**
The experiences of a highly dedicated civil rights lawyer chiefly in Southern courts.

(Y,J) Lacy, Leslie A. *Cheer the lonesome traveler: the life of W. E. B. DuBois.* **Dial, 1970. Paper.**
An interesting biography for young people.

(Y,J) Laye, Camara. *The dark child.* **Farrar, 1954. Paper.**
Autobiography of an African boy from French Guinea. Good reading for grades 7-12.

(J) Lee, Irvin. *Negro medal of honor men.* **Dodd, 1967.**
A history of Negro participation in all America's wars as told through the medium of the deeds of Negro Congressional Medal winners.

(Y,J) Lewis, Claude. *Benjamin Banneker: the man who saved Washington.* **McGraw, 1970.**
Young people's biography of a notable eighteenth century Negro scientist and designer.

(J) Lichello, Robert. *Pioneer in blood plasma: Dr. Charles Richard Drew.* **Messner, 1968.**
Story of the Negro scientist in the Second World War.

(A) Lincoln, C. Eric (ed.) *Martin Luther King, Jr.; a profile.* **Hill & Wang, 1970. Paper.**
Well-chosen selections from biographies and periodicals that together form a good all-round picture of the man and his work. Useful for any library.

(A) Little, Malcolm. *Malcolm X speaks.* **Merit Publishers, 1965. Paper.**
Speeches which shed light on the theories of Negro nationalism.

(A,Y) Lyons, Thomas T. *Black leadership in American history.* **Addison-Wesley Pub. Co., 1971. Paper.**
Biographical essays of about forty pages each of Douglass, Booker T. Washington, DuBois, Garvey and King. Good for high school libraries.

(A) Malcolm X. *Autobiography of Malcolm X.* **Grove, 1965. Paper.**
An important part of the history of recent Negro militancy. Should be read by all teachers of black studies.

(A) Mays, Benjamin E. *Born to rebel.* **Scribner, 1971.**
Autobiography of one of the country's outstanding black leaders, now President of the Board of Education of Atlanta.

(J) McNeer, May Yonge and Lynd Ward. *Give me freedom.* **Abingdon, 1964.**
Biographical sketches of noted Negroes, written for middle school readers.

(J) Meltzer, Milton. *Langston Hughes: a biography.* **Crowell, 1968.**
Appropriate for middle school readers.

(Y) Meltzer, Milton. *Thaddeus Stevens and the fight for Negro rights.* **Crowell, 1967.**
Good biography of a very controversial man who led the fight for Negro rights in the mid-nineteenth century.

(Y,J) Meltzer, Milton. *Tongue of flame; the life of Lydia Maria Child.* **Crowell, 1965.**
Biography of a noted abolitionist.

(A) Meredith, James. *Three years in Mississippi.* **Indiana Univ. Press, 1966.**
The author's own account of his successful fight to enter the state university, and his view of the whole racial situation.

(A) Merrill, Walter M. *Against wind and tide: a biography of William Lloyd Garrison.* **Harvard Univ. Press, 1963.**

(A,Y) Metcalf, George. *Black profiles.* **McGraw, 1968.**
Biographical sketches of eleven noted black leaders, past and present. Good for high school reference.

(Y) Miller, Floyd. *Ahdoolo: the biography of Matthew A. Henson.* **Dutton, 1963.**
Story of the Negro who accompanied Peary to the North Pole in 1909.

(A,Y) Moody, Anne. *Coming of age in Mississippi.* **Dial, 1968. Paper.**
Autobiography about a black woman's life in rural Mississippi from childhood to the days of civil rights warfare. Very readable.

(A) Moore, Jenny. *The people on Second Street.* **Morrow, 1968.**
Reminiscences of a clerical couple who spent eight years in a ghetto church in Jersey City, N. J., trying to help the neighborhood. Good reading.

(A) Morrow, E. Frederic. *Black man in the White House.* **Coward, 1963. Paper.**
Diary of the first Negro to be a Presidential assistant. He was an advisor on racial and civil rights matters in the Eisenhower administration.

(A) Neary, John. *Julian Bond, black rebel.* **Morrow, 1971.**
Biography of a contemporary Negro political figure.

(J) Nolan, Jeannette. *John Brown.* **Messner, 1950.**
A biography for junior school level readers.

(A) O'Daniel, Therman B. (ed.) *Langston Hughes, black genius.* **Morrow, 1971.**
Collection of essays by twelve writers, each dealing with some aspect of Hughes' life and work. Useful for teachers or other adults interested in Negro literature.

(Y) Orrmont, Arthur. *Fighter against slavery: Jehudi Ashmun.* **Messner, 1966.**
Biography of a young man who in the early nineteenth century became deeply involved in trying to abolish slavery in Africa, and took part in the founding of Liberia.

(A) Osofsky, Gilbert (comp.) *Puttin' on ole massa.* **Harper, 1969. Paper.**
Preceded by an excellent introductory essay, this book reprints the narratives written by three fugitive slaves. Very vivid and personal history.

(Y) Owens, Jesse. *The Jesse Owens story.* **Putnam, 1970.**
An interesting, inspiring autobiography which any young reader can enjoy.

(A,Y) Pauli, Hertha. *Her name was Sojourner Truth.* **Appleton, 1962.**
Biography of a noted nineteenth century black woman.

(J) Petry, Ann. *Harriet Tubman.* **Crowell, 1955. Paper.**

(Y,J) Pitrone, Jean. *Trailblazer; Negro nurse in the American Red Cross.* **Harcourt, 1969.**
Biography of the first Negro nurse in the Red Cross. Junior high school level.

(J) Preston, Edward. *Martin Luther King: fighter for freedom.* **Doubleday, 1968. Paper.**
A biography for junior high school level.

(A,Y) Proudfoot, Merrill. *Diary of a sit-in.* **Univ. of North Carolina Press, 1962. Paper.**
A personal record of a sit-in by students in Knoxville (1960) which after a few weeks desegregated lunch counters there. The author is a white professor and clergyman who helped lead the action.

(A) Quarles, Benjamin. *Frederick Douglass.* **Associated Publishers, 1948. Paper.**
An authoritative one-volume biography for adult readers.

(A) Reddick, Lawrence D. *Crusader without violence.* **Harper, 1959.**
A biography of Martin Luther King, Jr.

(A) Redding, J. Saunders. *On being Negro in America.* **Bobbs, 1951.**
A moving and valuable personal memoir by a noted Negro writer.

(A,Y) Richardson, Ben A. *Great American Negroes.* **Crowell, 1956.**
Collective biography.

(Y,J) Rollins, Charlemae. *Black troubadour.* **Rand McNally, 1970.**
The life of Langston Hughes, written for young people.

(Y) Rollins, Charlemae. *Famous American Negro poets.* Dodd, 1965. Paper.
Collective biographical sketches.

(J) Rollins, Charlemae. *They showed the way: forty American Negro leaders.* Crowell, 1964.
Biographical sketches of men and women who succeeded in a variety of careers.

(A) Rudwick, Elliott. *W. E. B. DuBois.* Univ. of Pennsylvania Press, 1960. Paper.
Biography and social analysis of his long career.

(A) Seale, Bobby. *Seize the time: the story of the Black Panther Party and Huey P. Newton.* Random, 1971. Paper.
Seale's account of his life and racial activism. Long, but easy reading. Suitable for any library.

(A) Simon, Paul. *Lovejoy, martyr to freedom.* Concordia, 1964.
Biography of the abolitionist leader.

(A) Smith, William G. *Return to black America.* Prentice, 1969.
Written by an expatriate American Negro, representing a French newspaper agency. It is a report of his visit in 1967 to black militant groups at the height of the activist period.

(A,Y) Spencer, Samuel R. *Booker T. Washington and the Negro's place in American life.* Little, 1955. Paper.
A fairly short biography for general and secondary school use.

(A) Stalvey, Lois M. *The education of a WASP.* Morrow, 1970. Paper.
Highly readable account of a middle-class woman from Nebraska who moved into a black Philadelphia ghetto.

(Y) Sterling, Dorothy. *Captain of the Planter; the story of Robert Smalls.* Doubleday, 1958. Paper.

(Y,J) Sterling, Dorothy. *Freedom train: the story of Harriet Tubman.* Doubleday, 1954.

(Y,J) Sterling, Dorothy. *Making of an Afro-American.* Doubleday, 1970. Paper.
Biography of Martin Robison Delaney (1812-1885), a leader among black abolitionists.

(J) Sterling, Dorothy and Benjamin Quarles. *Lift every voice.* Doubleday, 1965. Paper.
Biographical sketches of the lives of Booker T. Washington, W. E. B. DuBois, Mary Terrell and James Weldon Johnson.

(J) Sterling, Philip and Rayford Logan. *Four took freedom.* Doubleday, 1967. Paper.
Stories of four great Negro leaders who had been slaves — Harriet Tubman, Frederick Douglass, Robert Smalls and Blanche Bruce.

(Y,J) Sterne, Emma. *I have a dream.* Knopf, 1965.
Written especially for teen-agers, this is a collection of biographical sketches of some leading black Americans, such as Marian Anderson, Philip Randolph, Daisy Bates and James Farmer.

(J) Stevenson, Janet. *Soldiers in the civil rights war.* Reilly & Lee, 1970.
Biographies of a number of civil rights advocates from Thaddeus Stevens to Martin Luther King, Jr. Good junior high school material.

(J) Stratton, Madeline. *Negroes who helped build America.* Ginn, 1965.
Biographies of fourteen prominent Negroes past and present. Most useful for middle schools.

(A) Stringfellow, William. *My people is the enemy.* Holt, 1964. Paper.
A brief but well-written book by a White Protestant layman and lawyer who spent some years working in religious work in East Harlem. He gives his observations and thoughts.

(Y,J) Stull, Edith. *Unsung black Americans.* **Grosset & Dunlap, 1970.**
Short biographical sketches of a number of Negroes of note in history. Good supplementary reading or reference for schools.

(A) Sugarman, Tracy. *Stranger at the gates.* **Hill & Wang, 1966.**
The author is a Connecticut artist and illustrator who took part in the civil rights drive in Mississippi in 1964. This is his highly readable account of what went on that summer.

(Y) Swift, Hildegarde. *Railroad to freedom.* **Harcourt, 1952, 1960.**
A biography of Harriet Tubman.

(A,Y) Thomas, John L. *The liberator: William Lloyd Garrison.* **Little, 1963.**
A biography suitable for general reading.

(A) Thompson, Daniel C. *The Negro leadership class.* **Prentice, 1963.**
A serious study of seventy-five Negro leaders in New Orleans in the early 1960's — what they believed, how they functioned, and so on. College level.

(A) Thornbrough, Emma L. (ed.) *Black reconstructionists.* **Prentice, 1972 (Great Lives Observed Series).**
This is a worthwhile picture of the Negroes who gained public office in the decade after the Civil War. Many of them were far more capable than historians gave them credit for being. This book gives excerpts from articles about them and from their own words.

(Y) Thornbrough, Emma Lou. *Booker T. Washington* **(Great Lives Observed Series). Prentice, 1969. Paper.**

(Y) Toppin, Edgar A. *A mark well made.* **Rand McNally, 1967.**
Stories of outstanding American Negroes.

(A,Y) Truth, Sojourner. *Sojourner Truth; narrative and book of life.* **Johnson Pub. Co., 1970.**
Material about and by Sojourner Truth.

(A) Ullman, Victor. *Martin R. Delany: the beginnings of black national-ism.* Beacon, 1971.
Biography of a leading free Negro before the Civil War, who worked hard to establish an African colony for American blacks.

(A,Y) Wagenknecht, Edward C. *Harriet Beecher Stowe: the known and the unknown.* Oxford, 1965.
A biography for high school or general libraries.

(A) Ward, Hiley H. *Prophet of the black nation.* Pilgrim, 1969.
About the Rev. Albert Cleage, controversial black Detroit minister, who advocates the idea of Christianity as basically a black militant religion.

(A) Washington, Booker T. *Up from slavery.* Dodd, 1965. **Paper.**
A reprint of this famous autobiography.

(A) Waters, Ethel. *His eye is on the sparrow.* Doubleday, 1951. **Paper.**
An autobiography by this noted entertainer.

(A) Weatherby, William. *Love in the shadows.* Stein & Day, 1966.
A British journalist's account of his experiences in America seeking to understand the racial situation. Vivid, real and personal; good general reading.

(A) Weinberg, Meyer (ed.) *W. E. B. DuBois; a reader.* Harper, 1970.
Contains some eighty selections from DuBois' writings.

(A) Weinberg, Kenneth G. *Black victory; Carl Stokes and the winning of Cleveland.* Quadrangle, 1968.
A biography of the first Negro to be elected mayor of a major American city.

(J) Weiner, Sandra. *It's wings that make birds fly.* Pantheon, 1968.
A real-life story of a ten-year old Negro boy in a ghetto, written from taped interviews and photographs. A vivid picture, suitable for elementary school class discussions.

(J) White, Anne T. *George Washington Carver.* Random, 1953.
A biography for young people.

(A) Williams, John A. *The King God didn't save.* Coward, 1970.
A book about Martin Luther King, Jr., and especially why he was killed. The implication is that he was the victim of a white conspiracy.

(A) Williams, John A. *This is my country too.* New American Library, 1965. Paper.
Account of the Negro author's eight-month trip around the United States a decade ago. Shows the many difficulties and discrimnations he met. Subjective and rather bitter.

(J) Wise, William. *Booker T. Washington.* Putnam, 1968.

(J) Woodson, Carter G. and Charles Wesley. *Negro makers of history.* Associated Publishers, 1958.
For junior high school students.

(A) Wright, Richard. *Black boy.* Harper, 1945. Paper.
An autobiography by this noted writer.

(Y) Young, Margaret. *Black American leaders.* Watts, 1969.
Collection of biographical sketches.

PART III

ESSAYS, ANTHOLOGIES, BOOKS ON CURRENT PROBLEMS

OF THE NEGRO IN AMERICA

(Y) Adoff, Arnold (comp.) *Black on black; commentaries by Negro Americans.* **Macmillan, 1968. Paper.**
Excerpts from the writings of twenty-three Negro authors, past and present. They are well-chosen to show that current Negro protest is only a more outspoken way of expressing what Negroes have always felt.

(A) Alex, Nicholas. *Black in blue; a study of the Negro policeman.* **Appleton, 1969. Paper.**
Sociological study of black members of New York City's police force. Based largely on interviews, quoted at length. Interesting general reading.

(A) Aptheker, Herbert. *Soul of the republic: the Negro today.* **Marzani & Munsell, 1964.**
A brief book, highly pro-Negro and anti-establishment, surveying black conditions in each state in 1961 as reported in the series of commission reports on civil rights authorized by Congress.

(A,Y) Ashmore, Harry S. *The other side of Jordan.* **Norton, 1960.**
Written by a noted Southern newspaper editor, this book is an expanded version of twelve articles he wrote for national syndication, dealing with the problems of Negroes in northern cities in 1960. Easy to read, revealing and sympathetic.

(A) Baker, Ray Stannard. *Following the color line.* **Harper, 1908; Harper Torch Book, 1964. Paper.**
Contains the series of articles written by Baker in the 1900's for *The American Magazine.* They constituted one of the first and best studies of the race problem to be written for the general public. Progressive and objective for the period when they were written.

(A,Y) Baldwin, James. *The fire next time.* **Dial, 1963. Paper.**
Essays on the race question, emphasizing the need for racial cooperation, not separatism.

(A,Y) Baldwin, James. *Nobody knows my name; more notes of a native son.* **Dial, 1961. Paper.**
Essays by one of the best Negro writers; they deal with a wide variety of topics relating to Negro culture and problems. Worthwhile reading for adults or high school students.

(A) Baldwin, James. *Notes of a native son.* **Beacon, 1955. Paper.**
A collection of ten essays by Baldwin, written at different times and on as many phases of the Negro experience in America, and on his own years as an expatriate in Paris.

(A) Banton, Michael. *Race relations.* **Basic Books, 1968.**
Scholarly study of world-wide racial problems.

(A) Barbour, Floyd B. (comp.) *The Black Power revolt.* **Sargent, 1968. Paper.**
A collection of brief essays and position papers about the identity of Negroes as a race — the Black Power concept. All the writers are Negroes, most of them well-known. They range from Turner and Douglass to Carmichael and LeRoi Jones.

(A) Bell, Inge P. *CORE and the strategy of non-violence.* **Random, 1968. Paper.**

(A) Bennett, Lerone, Jr. *The black mood.* **Johnson Pub. Co., 1964. Paper.**
Essays on the Negro outlook on their problems.

(A) Bennett, Lerone, Jr. *Challenge of blackness.* **Johnson Pub. Co., 1972.**
Essays and speeches about the black thrust for political, cultural and economic status in America.

(A) Bernstein, Saul. *Alternatives to violence.* **Association Press, 1967. Paper.**
About hostile youth in nine major cities. It describes their troubles and prejudices as revealed by interviews.

(A) Boesel, David and Peter Rossi. *Cities under siege: an anatomy of the ghetto riots, 1964-1968.* **Basic Books, 1971.**
Case studies of five urban riots—Newark, Plainfield, Los Angeles, Milwaukee and Cambridge, Maryland. These are followed by fifteen essays on the social and political implications, by various writers. Good adult reading.

(A) Boggs, James. *Racism and the class struggle.* **Monthly Review, 1970.**
Essays and speeches about the black revolution in America, of which the writer is a strong advocate.

(A) Bowen, David. *The struggle within; race relations in the United States.* **Norton, 1965.**
An analysis of the race problem.

(Y,J) Boyle, Sarah. *For human beings only; a primer of human understanding.* **Seabury, 1964. Paper.**
A good useful book for learning and teaching about racial prejudice. For junior and senior high schools.

(A) Brazier, Arthur M. *Black self-determination.* **Eerdmans, 1968.**
The author is a Chicago minister and a leader in trying to involve churches in helping Negroes to achieve racial solidarity and power without separatism. He believes the present social structure must be altered.

(A) Brickman, William W. and Stanley Lehrer (eds.) *The countdown on segregated education.* **Society for the Advancement of Education, 1960.**
Interesting and useful study of the question of school segregation.

(A) Brink, William and Louis Harris. *Black and white; a study of U.S. racial attitudes today.* **Clarion, 1969. Paper.**
Results of a survey taken several years after the authors' 1963 study, both in conjunction with *Newsweek.*

(A) Brink, William and Louis Harris. *The Negro revolution in America.* **Simon & Schuster, 1964. Paper.**
A thorough report of an opinion poll taken in 1963 by *Newsweek* and the Harris poll organization. Some 250 questions were asked of more than a thousand Negroes over the country, and of an equal number of whites. This book describes and analyzes the results, and also lists the questions and statistical scores.

(A,Y) Broderick, Francis and August Meier (eds.) *Negro protest thought in the twentieth century.* (The American Heritage Series). Bobbs, 1965. Paper.
A collection of fifty writings of black leaders from Booker T. Washington to Martin Luther King, Jr. and James Farmer. Each is introduced by a brief explanatory editorial statement. Good reference source at any level.

(A) Broom, Leonard and Norval Glenn. *Transformation of the American Negro.* Harper, 1965. Paper.
A social analysis in less than 200 pages of the many aspects of Negro attempts to fit into a society which has too often rejected them. While written by professional sociologists, the book is directed at the general reader.

(A,Y) Burns, W. Hayward. *The voices of Negro protest in America.* Oxford Univ. Press, 1963.
A summary of current Negro efforts for equality, through various organizations and movements.

(A,Y) Caldwell, Erskine. *In search of Bisco.* Farrar, 1965.
Thoughts on racism in the Deep South by a noted writer who is both Southern and anti-segregationist. Good reading for either adults or secondary schools.

(A) Canty, Donald. *A single society; alternatives to urban apartheid.* Praeger, 1969. Paper.
Serious discussion of ways to eliminate segregation in communities in the future.

(A) Carmichael, Peter A. *The South and segregation.* Public Affairs Press, 1965.
A serious and scholarly book which strongly condemns the Supreme Court for its 1954 school segregation decision. Interesting reading for an informed adult.

(A) Carmichael, Stokely and Charles Hamilton. *Black power.* Random, 1967. Paper.
A description and rationale for the Black Power movement. Useful mainly for the record, in view of Carmichael's notoriety.

(A) Carson, Josephine. *Silent voices.* **Delacorte, 1969.**
A documentary study of Southern Negro women whom the author talked with about their race problems and opinions.

(A) Clark, Kenneth B. *Dark ghetto; dilemmas of social power.* **Harper, 1965. Paper.**
Serious study of Harlem, of ghetto psychology and the impact of the civil rights movement.

(A) Clark, Kenneth B. *The Negro protest.* **Beacon, 1963.**
Three interviews recorded for a television program in which Dr. Clark talks with Martin Luther King, Jr., James Baldwin and Malcolm X. A realistic appraisal of these men.

(A) Clarke, John H. *Harlem, a community in transition.* **Citadel, 1964. Paper.**

(A) Cleage, Albert B. *The black Messiah.* **Sheed & Ward, 1968. Paper.**
Sermons to blacks about Christianity as a black historical movement; strongly militant point-of-view about world conditions.

(A) Cleaver, Eldridge. *Post-prison writings and speeches.* **(Edited by Robert Scheer). Random, 1969. Paper.**
Reflections on black America by one of the chief leaders of the Black Panther party.

(A) Clift, Virgil A., A. W. Anderson and H. G. Hullfish (eds.) *Negro education in America* **(16th yearbook of the John Dewey Society). Harper, 1962.**
Twelve essays divided into four parts: background, the problem, effects of the Brown decision, and the future outlook. For adult students.

(A) Cohen, Jerry and William S. Murphy. *Burn, baby burn!* **Dutton, 1966.**
Analysis of the Watts riot of 1965.

(A) Coles, Robert. *Farewell to the South.* **Little, 1972.**
A collection of his articles and essays, written over a period of time, and based on his many interviews with members of both races in the South. An excellent portrait of a people.

(Y,J) Coles, Robert. *The image is you.* **Houghton, 1969.**
A collection of ghetto pictures taken by children accompanied by a text and some taped interviews. The total comprises a portrait of black slum life. Probably of most interest to young people in similar environments.

(A) Coles, Robert. *Uprooted children; the early life of migrant farm workers.* **Univ. of Pittsburgh Press, 1970. Paper.**
Personal experiences of a noted authority in the study of poverty. An important book for adults concerned with the poorest social conditions.

(A) Comer, James P. *Beyond black and white.* **Quadrangle, 1972.**
Analysis of the origins and development of racial conflict in the United States, and how our social institutions tend to perpetuate it.

(A) Commager, Henry S. (ed.) *The struggle for racial equality.* **Harper, 1967.**
Thirty-eight excerpts of writings, speeches, etc., important to the civil rights cause. Makes generally interesting reading, with good editorial notes.

(A) Conant, James B. *Slums and suburbs.* **McGraw, 1961. Paper.**
Analytical comparison of schools in ghettos and suburbs. Controversial but stimulating ideas.

(A) Cook, James G. *The segregationists.* **Appleton, 1962.**
Written by a Southern United Press reporter, this is a very interesting personal description of a wide variety of individuals and groups in the South that fought integration.

(A) Corson, William R. *Promise or peril; the black college student in America.* **Norton, 1970.**
The writer, basing his thoughts on wide experience with war, revolution and violence over the world, believes that unless America can keep the black college students from being captured by the militants, revolution is inevitable. Valuable reading for adults.

(A) Cox, Archibald, *et al.* *Civil rights, the Constitution and the courts.* **Harvard Univ. Press, 1967.**
Three lectures given in 1965-66 by Cox, Mark D. Howe and J. R. Wiggins.

(A) Cox, Oliver C. *Caste, class and race.* Monthly Review Press, 1959. Paper.
A long scholarly work on the broad subject of racial prejudice in the world. Good background for teachers.

(A) Crain, Robert L. *Politics of school desegregation.* Aldine, 1968. Paper.
A study of the relationships between the racial reorganization of schools and the political power structure of the community. Specific cases are studied in a number of cities, north and south.

(A) Cross, Theodore L. *Black capitalism; strategy for business in the ghetto.* Atheneum, 1969.
A white businessman offers practical solutions to the economic problems of the inner city.

(A) Cruse, Harold. *Crisis of the Negro intellectual.* Morrow, 1967. Paper.
Analysis of individuals and of the organizations they joined or led.

(A) Cruse, Harold. *Rebellion or revolution?* Morrow, 1968. Paper.
Study of the racial impasse in America, with reference to the ideas and objectives of various Negro leaders.

(A) Culbertson, Judi and Patti Bard. *The little white book on race.* Lippincott, 1970. Paper.
An amusing satirical book about white racial "moderates." Fun about prejudice.

(A) Curry, Gladys J. (ed.) *Viewpoints from black America.* Prentice, 1970. Paper.
Collection of prose pieces, intended chiefly as a reader for college composition.

(A) Curtis, James C. and Lewis Gould (eds.) *The black experience in America.* Univ. of Texas Press, 1969. Paper.
Contains eight essays based on a series of lectures given at the University of Texas, and dealing with a wide range of subjects in black history.

(A) Dabbs, James M. *The Southern heritage.* **Knopf, 1958.**
Written by an intelligent and understanding Southerner, this book analyzes the background and reasons for the South's views on race.

(A) Damerell, Reginald. *Triumph in a white suburb.* **Morrow, 1968. Paper.**
A detailed report of how, in Teaneck, N. J., citizens overcame both a ghetto housing factor and de facto school segregation.

(A) Daniel, Bradford (ed.) *Black, white and grey.* **Sheed & Ward, 1964.**
Collection of twenty-one writings on the civil rights problem by a variety of people with different points of view — Roy Wilkins, Orval Faubus, King and many others. Stimulating and useful because of the outspoken differences.

(A) Davis, Angela. *If they come in the morning.* **Third Press, 1972.**
Highly personal and subjective expression of the idea of "political imprisonment," both in her own and other cases.

(A) Dollard, John. *Caste and class in a southern town.* **Doubleday, 1957. Paper.**
Interviews with blacks and whites.

(A) Drake, St. Clair and Horace Cayton. *Black metropolis; a study of Negro life in a northern city.* **Harper, 1962. Paper.**
An outstanding social survey in this field. The setting is Chicago.

(A) DuBois, W. E. B. *"The Crisis"* writings **(edited by Daniel Walden). Fawcett, 1972. Paper.**
Contains over 400 pages of articles and editorials written by Dr. DuBois for *The Crisis* from 1910 to 1934. This journal was the voice of the NAACP, and DuBois was its editor. This book contains some of the best writing extant on the problems of race in this country.

(A) Dunbar, Ernest. *Black expatriates.* **Dutton, 1968. Paper.**
Consists of reports of interviews with sixteen American Negroes who left America to live in Africa or Western Europe. All of them are professionals, of one sort or another; and their thinking is interesting. The author and interviewer was a Negro editor of *Look.*

(A) *Ebony. White on black.* Johnson Pub. Co., 1963.
Views about Negroes written by twenty-two white Americans.

(A) *Ebony.* (eds.) *White problem in America.* Johnson Pub. Co., 1966.
Paper.
Twenty-one essays previously published in *Ebony* in 1965 by leading Negro writers. Stresses the Negro attitude toward white
responsibility for solution of the race question.

(A,Y) Edwards, Harry. *Revolt of the black athlete.* Free Press, 1969.
Paper.
The author is a black professor of social studies who led an effort
to get black athletes to boycott the 1968 Olympics. This book
shows how racial prejudice enters into all fields of sport. While
of course it is highly subjective, it is a valuable revelation and
well worth reading.

(A) Ellis, William W. *White ethics and black power.* Aldine, 1969.
A report on the West Side Organization of Chicago, and a criti-
cism of white political attitudes.

(A) Etzkowitz, Henry and Gerald Schoflander. *Ghetto crisis: riots or
reconciliation?* Little, 1969.
The authors are white sociologists who in 1967 established a
community co-op center in the Bedford-Stuyvesant ghetto of
Brooklyn. This tells about the experiment.

(A) Fanon, Frantz. *Black skin, white masks.* Grove, 1967. Paper.
First published in France, written by a psychiatrist born in Mar-
tinique. The book is an interesting, if highly subjective, study of
black feeling.

(A) Farmer, James. *Freedom when?* Random, 1965.
Very readable account of the civil rights movement by a noted
Negro leader who was a founder and director of CORE.

(A) Ferman, Louis A. (comp.) *Negroes and jobs; a book of readings.*
Univ. of Michigan Press, 1968. Paper.
Contains some thirty articles selected from various sources. Deals
with causes and extent of Negro disadvantages in employment.

(A) Foner, Philip S. (ed.) *The Black Panthers speak.* Lippincott, 1970. Paper.
Contains the official manifesto of the party and statements of belief and purpose by such leaders as Seale, Cleaver and Newton.

(A) Forman, Robert E. *Black ghettos, white ghettos and slums.* Prentice, 1972.
Adult sociological study of poverty urban areas and their relation to racism. The author is a professor at the University of Toledo.

(A) Frazier, Edward Franklin. *Black bourgeoisie.* Macmillan, 1957. Paper.
The best study of middle-class Negroes.

(A) Frazier, Edward Franklin. *Negro church in America.* Schocken, 1963. Paper.
Scholarly study of the evolution of Negro churches in America.

(A) Frazier, Edward Franklin. *Negro family in the United States.* Univ. of Chicago Press, 1966. Paper.
An important and valuable study of black family life.

(A,Y) Freed, Leonard. *Black in white America.* Grossman, 1969. Paper.
A collection of excellent human interest photographs depicting aspects of Negro life in America, with a well-written text sympathetic to the Negro cause.

(A,Y) Friedman, Leon (ed.) *The civil rights reader.* Walker & Co., 1967. Paper.
A varied and generally interesting collection of book excerpts, speeches, court opinions and other materials. Much of these can be profitably used for student reading.

(A) Friedman, Leon (ed.) *Southern justice.* Pantheon, 1965. Paper.
Nineteen lawyers write chapters on various aspects of the racial abuse of law by some Southern courts and legislatures. It is an angry book, specific in names and cases. Makes interesting reading and is well documented.

(Y,J) Froman, Robert. *Racism.* Delacorte, 1970.
Explains the differences between race and racism.

(A) Fullinwider, S. P. *The mind and mood of black America.* **Dorsey, 1969. Paper.**
Discusses Negro thinking in the twentieth century.

(A) Gayle, Addison, Jr. *The black situation.* **Dell, 1970. Paper.**
Discusses Negro attitudes toward the various solutions proposed by black groups.

(A) Geltman, Max. *The confrontation: black power, anti-semitism and the myth of integration.* **Prentice, 1970.**
Good adult reading, dealing with the causes of ghetto riots, the sociology of Negro families and the Negro-Jewish conflict.

(A) Geschwender, James A. (ed.) *The black revolt.* **Prentice, 1971.**
Anthology of scholarly essays dealing with the history of the civil rights movement, ghetto uprisings and black separatism.

(A) Ginsberg, Eli (ed.) *Business leadership and the Negro crisis.* **McGraw, 1969.**
Speeches by white and black business leaders at a conference at Columbia University in 1968. Useful for students of the economics of the race question.

(A) Ginsberg, Eli. *The Negro challenge to the business community.* **McGraw, 1964. Paper.**

(A) Ginsberg, Eli, *et al.* The Negro potential. **Columbia Univ. Press, 1956. Paper.**
Important report on the possibilities of economic improvement for Negroes.

(A) Goldman, Peter. *Report from black America.* **Simon & Schuster, 1970.**
Study of Negro reactions to current social problems.

(A) Gossett, Thomas F. *Race; the history of an idea in America.* **Southern Methodist Univ. Press, 1963. Paper.**
An interesting and scholarly study of the reasons for racism, its various manifestations, and the scientific arguments about it over the years.

71

(A,Y) Greeley, Andrew M. *Why can't they be like us?* **Dutton, 1971.**
A report on the views and beliefs of white ethnic groups.

(A) Greenberg, Jack. *Race relations and the American law.* **Columbia Univ. Press, 1959.**
Serious scholarly analysis. Research or reference.

(A) Greene, Mary F. and Orletta Ryan. *Schoolchildren growing up in the slums.* **Pantheon, 1966.**
Anecdotal accounts of the authors' experiences with young ghetto children in Harlem.

(A) Gregory, Dick. *The shadow that scares me.* **Doubleday, 1968. Paper.**
A series of ten essays or chapters on the necessity of the Negro's true place in American society being recognized. He does not speak for the black revolutionary but for the Negro with a strong moral cause.

(A) Grier, William H. and Price Cobbs. *Black rage.* **Basic Books, 1968. Paper.**
Written by two psychiatrists, this is a serious, pessimistic study of black hopelessness in a white society.

(A) Grier, William H. and Price Cobbs. *The Jesus bag.* **McGraw, 1971.**
Discusses the meaning of Christianity to blacks, and holds that black morality derived from it should be adopted by the whole country.

(A,Y) Grier, William H. and Price Cobbs. *Why do they act that way?* **Bantam, 1970. Paper.**
A study of the causes of the ills of young blacks.

(A) Groh, George W. *The black migration: the journey to urban America.* **McKay, 1972.**
Studies the many serious problems caused by the mass migration of Negroes from the South to Northern cities.

(A) Handlin, Oscar. *Fire-bell in the night: the crisis in civil rights.* **Little, 1964. Paper.**
A brief series of essays by a noted historian, examining the future of the race question.

(A) Handlin, Oscar. *The newcomers: Negroes and Puerto Ricans in a changing metropolis.* Harvard Univ. Press, 1959. **Paper.**
A study of racial problems in the New York metropolitan area.

(A,Y) Hentoff, Nat. *The new equality.* Viking, 1964. **Paper.**
Interesting account of the whole gamut of race problems as they existed in the early 1960's.

(A) Hernton, Calvin C. *White papers for white Americans.* Doubleday, 1966.
Several serious essays on the race problem in America. The author tries to bring home to the white society the real seriousness of the racial situation.

(A) Hesslink, George. *Black neighbors; Negroes in a northern rural community.* Bobbs, 1968. **Paper.**
Sociological study of Cass County, Michigan, in a unique area in which true equality and stability among Negroes and whites have developed.

(A) Hill, Norman (ed.) *The Black Panther menace.* Popular Library, 1971. **Paper.**
Collection of articles by several writers who see the Panthers as neo-Nazis. Very readable.

(A) Hill, Roy L. (ed.) *Rhetoric of racial revolt.* Golden Bell Press, 1964.
A collection of speeches given at various dates by Negro leaders ranging from Douglass to King and Malcolm X. The editor provides a good analysis.

(A) Humphrey, Hubert H. (ed.) *Integration vs. segregation.* Crowell, 1964.
A good collection of documents and essays from many sources; intended for supplementary use in courses dealing with interracial education.

(A) Isaacs, Harold R. *New world of Negro Americans.* Day, 1963.
An interesting study of the impact of emerging Africa on the American Negro's image of himself as someone with an identity in the world.

(A,Y) Isenberg, Irwin (ed.) *The city in crisis.* **H. W. Wilson, 1968 (Vol. 40, No. 1 of** *The Reference Shelf***).**
Useful collection of excerpts from newspaper and magazine articles. Good supplementary reading.

(A) Jacobs, Paul. *Prelude to riot.* **Random, 1967. Paper.**
The author describes vividly his intensive investigation of the condition in the Los Angeles Negro slums. He deals with politics, education, housing, health and many other problems, typical of many other cities.

(A) Johnson, Haynes B. *Dusk at the mountain.* **Doubleday, 1963.**
Written by a white newspaperman, this is a very readable and sympathetic picture of the Negroes of Washington, D. C.

(A) Jones, LeRoi. *Home: social essays.* **Morrow, 1966. Paper.**
About two dozen essays on aspects of black problems. Although they are, of course, highly subjective, they are worthwhile reading.

(A) Kain, John F. (ed.) *Race and poverty.* **Prentice, 1970. Paper.**
Twenty-one excerpts from recent scholarly writing dealing in various ways with the economics of discrimination.

(A) Killens, John C. *Black man's burden.* **Simon & Schuster, 1965. Paper.**
A Negro statement of the racial situation as he sees it — the need for Negro leadership to overcome racism.

(A) Killian, Lewis M. *The impossible revolution: black power and the American dream.* **Random, 1968. Paper.**
An analysis of Black Power and its white opponents. The author sees little likelihood of an adjustment, and forecasts serious trouble.

(A) Killian, Lewis and Charles Grigg. *Racial crisis in America; leadership in conflict.* **Prentice, 1964. Paper.**
Short, scholarly study of race relations and of alternative outcomes.

(A) Kilpatrick, James J. *Southern case for school segregation.* **Collier, 1962.**
The author is a leading Southern editor. This book tries to show the Southern arguments for segregation, although the author admits they must eventually lose.

(A) King, Martin Luther, Jr. *The trumpet of conscience.* Harper, 1968.
Five lectures showing King's philosophy shortly before his death.

(A) King, Martin Luther, Jr. *Where do we go from here: chaos or community?* Harper, 1967. Paper.
An important exposition of non-violence as a necessary procedure in Negro advance.

(A) Ladner, Joyce. *Tomorrow's tomorrow; the black woman.* Doubleday, 1971. Paper.
Study of the opinions of girls in black communities concerning their hopes for the future.

(A) Lecky, Robert S. and H. E. Wright (eds.) *Black manifesto; religion, racism and reparations.* Sheed & Ward, 1969. Paper.
The most important book on the subject of Negro reparation demands. Contains the text of Forman's Manifesto of 1969 and commentaries by several scholars, as well as the textual replies of churches. The general tone is basically sympathetic toward reparations.

(A) Lee, Frank F. *Negro and white in Connecticut Town.* Bookman Associates, 1961. Paper.
A study of race relations in a small Northern industrial town. Gives an interesting picture of the problems.

(A) Lester, Julius. *Look out, Whitey! black power's gonna get your mama!* Dail, 1968. Paper.
A highly personal history of the Black Power movement and SNCC by the latter's field secretary. Valuable as a statement of the position and prophecies of militant blacks.

(A) Lincoln, C. Eric (ed.) *Is anybody listening to black America?* Seabury, 1968. Paper.
A selected collection of brief excerpts from a wide variety of sources, expressing an equally wide range of points-of-view on the race question. One section cites Negro leaders, another ordinary black people, and the third white Americans. Good material for discussion groups.

(A) Lincoln, C. Eric. *My face is black.* Beacon, 1964.
A brief discussion of the moods and philosophy of modern blacks, especially the militants.

(A) Lincoln, C. Eric. *Sounds of the struggle.* **Morrow, 1967. Paper.**
Contains eighteen essays from various journals dealing with several aspects of civil rights, the Black Muslims, and the religious aspects of Negro problems. For general reading.

(A) Littleton, Arthur C. and Mary Burger (eds.) *Black viewpoints.* **New American Library, 1971. Paper.**
Excerpts from writings of some thirty black people from Douglass to the present.

(A) Lubell, Samuel. *White and black: test of a nation.* **Harper, 1964. Paper.**
Written by an important public opinion expert, this is a sound exposition of what North and South can each do about its racial problems.

(A) Mack, Raymond W. (ed.) *Prejudice and race relations.* **Quadrangle, 1970.**
Collection of articles on the racial crisis in America and elsewhere.

(A) Major, Reginald. *A panther is a black cat.* **Morrow, 1971.**
A rather militant account of the origins and doctrines of the Black Panther movement.

(A) Malcolm X. *The speeches of Malcolm X at Harvard.* **Morrow, 1968. Paper.**
These are talks given by the Black Muslim leader in 1961 and 1964, explaining his race feelings and his violent approach.

(A) Marino, Gene. *The Black Panthers.* **New American Library, 1969. Paper.**
An interesting descriptive account.

(A) Marrow, Alfred. *Changing patterns of prejudice.* **Chilton, 1962.**
An interesting book about racial and religious prejudice, especially in New York City, as it affects Jews, Negroes and Puerto Ricans.

(A) Marshall, F. Ray. *The Negro and organized labor.* **Wiley, 1965.**
A scholarly and thorough study of this relationship.

(A) Marx, Cary T. *Protest and prejudice; a study of belief in the black community.* Harper, 1967. Paper.
Report of an extensive survey of Negro opinion about themselves, their attitudes toward whites, and toward their many problems. Anti-Semitism among blacks is a particular concern of the study. This is a serious book, with many statistics, well worth the time of anyone wanting this kind of information.

(A) Masotti, Lewis H. and Don R. Bowen (eds.) *Riots and rebellion; Civil violence in the urban community.* Sage, 1969. Paper.
Collection of articles on urban violence.

(A) McCord, William, John Howard, Bernard Friedberg and Edwin Harwood. *Life styles in the black ghetto.* Norton, 1969. Paper.
A sociological study of urban conditions, making much use of interviews and polling techniques.

(A) McGill, Ralph. *The South and the Southerner.* Little, 1963. Paper.
Recollections and observations about the racial situation in the South by the noted publisher of *The Atlanta Constitution.* Enlightened comment, and very worthwhile.

(A) McKissick, Floyd. *Three-fifths of a man.* Macmillan, 1969.
A strong polemic for black economic power and the end of racism, with the argument that real enforcement of the Constitution is the only necessity.

(A) Mead, Margaret and James Baldwin. *A rap on race.* Lippincott, 1971.
A taped discussion between these two noted writers. Adult and highly interesting.

(A) Meier, August and Elliott Rudwick (eds.) *Black protest in the Sixties.* Quadrangle, 1970. Paper.
Collection of essays.

(A) Morgan, Charles. *A time to speak.* Harper, 1964.
A Birmingham lawyer condemns his city's stand on integration.

(A) Morris, Willie (ed.) *The South today, 100 years after Appomattox.* Harper, 1965.
Eleven essays by as many writers on various aspects of the South today. Most of them originally appeared in Harper's, of which Morris was formerly the editor.

(A) Morris, Willie. *Yazoo: integration in a Deep Southern town.* Harpers Magazine Press, 1971.
The author returns to his home town to report on racial conditions today.

(A) Moss, James A. (ed.) *The black man in America: integration and separation.* Delta, 1970. Paper.
Essays by contemporary Negro leaders.

(A) Mosteller, Frederick and Daniel P. Moynihan. *On equality of educational opportunity.* Random, 1972.
Papers derived from a Harvard seminar studying the Coleman Report, a Congressionally authorized survey of educational opportunity. Important, scholarly and very important to any adult concerned with the topic.

(A) Nelson, Truman J. *The right of revolution.* Beacon, 1968. Paper.
A polemical book by a white historian who seems to believe that revolution can be the only solution to racialism.

(A) Newby, Idus A. *Challenge to the court.* Louisiana State Univ. Press, 1967.
A study of segregationist literature since 1954. Shows the basic arguments and attitudes of those who defend racism and Negro inferiority. The writer's point-of-view, however, is liberal.

(A) Newman, Edwin. *The hate reader.* Oceana, 1964. Paper.
An interesting report and analysis of racial and political prejudice in the United States, giving many specific examples.

(A) Newton, Huey P. *To die for the people.* Vintage, 1972. Paper.
A collection of his essays and speeches.

(A) Norris, Hoke (ed.) *We dissent.* **St. Martins, 1962.**

Thirteen essays by Southern white Protestants selected by Norris, who are opposed to the rabid racist attitudes of many Southerners. The writers are not necessarily pro-Negro or anti-segregationist.

(A) Pantell, Dora and Edwin Greenidge. *If not now, when? the many meanings of black power.* **Delacorte, 1969.**

A discussion of the subject of "black power" for general reading.

(A) Parsons, Talcott and Kenneth Clark (eds.) *The Negro American.* **Houghton, 1966. Paper.**

Thirty essays by noted scholars and civil rights leaders, which together form an excellent study of the Negro problem.

(A) Petroni, Frank A. and Ernest Hirsch. *Two, four, six, eight, when you gonna integrate?* **Behavioral Publications, 1970. Paper.**

Sociological study of the reactions of white and black high school students. Mostly reports of student interviews. Good material for teachers.

(A) Porter, Judith D. *Black child, white child; the development of racial attitudes.* **Harvard Univ. Press, 1971.**

Scholarly study of young children, aged 3 to 5. Useful for teachers with some background in sociology and psychology.

(A) Powdermaker, Hortense. *After freedom.* **Atheneum, 1968. Paper.**

Originally published in 1939, this is a notable sociological study made of racial conditions and relationships in a Mississippi town.

(A) Powledge, Fred. *Black power, white resistance.* **World, 1967.**

Study of the racial situation by a white Southern reporter.

(A) Proctor, Samuel D. *The young Negro in America, 1960-1980.* **Association Press, 1966.**

The author is a man of wide experience with young people and with the race problem. Here he presents his ideas, hopefully, for the future of young blacks.

(A) Quarles, Benjamin (ed.) *Blacks on John Brown.* Univ. of Illinois Press, 1972.

An anthology of two dozen pieces — essays, poems, editorials and other writings — written by black authors about John Brown, who was a hero to the Negro people of his time and since.

(A) *Racism and American education.* Harper, 1970.

Report of a series of discussions on the subject by twenty prominent people, acting at the request of the Commission for the Observance of Human Rights Year (1968). Contains many valuable thoughts and proposals.

(A) Rainwater, Lee. *Behind ghetto walls; black families in a federal slum.* Aldine, 1970.

A serious study by the co-author of the Moynihan Report. Of interest to sociology students, etc.

(A) Reimers, David M. *White Protestantism and the Negro.* Oxford Univ. Press, 1965.

A study of the racial attitudes and practices of white Protestant churches. Chiefly for special interest readers.

(A) Robinson, James H. (ed.) *Love of this land.* Christian Education Press, 1956.

A collection of eight essays by various writers, each discussing Negro progress in a different field of interest: education, religion, business, sports, etc. Good general reading.

(A) Rose, Peter I. (ed.) *Americans from Africa.* (2 vols.: I, *Slavery and its aftermath;* II, *Old memories, new moods.*) Atherton, 1970.

An anthology of some 900 pages, of essays and other writing from many sources, on all phases of the black experience. An excellent library resource at any level.

(A,Y) Rose, Peter. *They and we.* Random, 1964. Paper.

Very useful little book on the history of race prejudice in this country, and on the causes and types of prejudice and discrimination. Good background material for any school library.

(A) Rosen, Harry and David. *But not next door.* Obolensky, 1962.

Interesting short study of the problem of segregated housing. Uses a partially fictional approach but the basic material is authentic.

(A) Ross, Arthur and Herbert Hill (eds.) *Employment, race and poverty.* Harcourt, 1965. Paper.
Collection of twenty excellent scholarly papers dealing with several aspects of the Negro labor and employment problem.

(A) Rubinstein, Annette (ed.) *Schools against children.* Monthly Review, 1969. Paper.
This contains a number of essays on the subject of community control of schools in large cities, chiefly New York. It provides good background for an understanding of the problem, but is rather one-sided (anti-school board) in its handling of the New York situation.

(A) Schanche, Don A. *The Panther paradox.* Paperback Library, 1971. Paper.
A generally sympathetic study of the Black Panthers, but recognizing their dangers. Especially useful for portraits of Cleaver, Seale and Newton.

(Y) Schechter, Betty. *The peaceable revolution.* Houghton, 1963.
Describes three kinds of "peaceable revolutions," — Thoreau's, Gandhi's and that of the Negroes of America.

(A) Schuchter, Arnold. *White power, black freedom.* Beacon, 1968. Paper.
A serious study of racial problems in cities, with some suggested solutions. A long serious book for the adult student.

(A,Y) Scott, Robert L. and Wayne Brockriede (comps.) *Rhetoric of black power.* Harper, 1969. Paper.
Thirteen excerpts from writing and speeches of several persons active in this field. Concentrates on aspects of black militancy.

(A,Y) Senser, Robert. *Primer on interracial justice.* Helicon, 1962. Paper.
A brief book dealing with the meaning and effects of racism and segregation. Easy to read; for public or school libraries.

(A) Silberman, Charles. *Crisis in black and white.* Random, 1964. Paper.
A study of integration and racial equality, and of the devastating effects of three hundred years of humiliation. Takes a pessimistic view of the future.

(A) Silver, James W. *Mississippi: the closed society.* **Harcourt, 1964. Paper.**
Written by a native of Mississippi, a professor of history there. Half the book vividly describes the James Meredith affair. The remainder consists of his own analysis of the "closed society" and of his correspondence with friends and critics of his anti-racist position. Lively reading.

(A,Y) Silverman, Sondra (comp.) *The black revolt and democratic politics.* **Heath, 1970. Paper.**
A brief book of readings and excerpts from well-known current writers. Useful supplementary reading with bibliography.

(A) Smith, Frank E. *Look away from Dixie.* **Louisiana State Univ. Press, 1965. Paper.**
Five essays by a former liberal Southern Congressman. His thesis is that the South must give up its provincial points-of-view and "join the mainstream of American life."

(A) Sowell, Thomas. *Black education: myths and tragedies.* **McKay, 1972.**
Study of the problems being faced, or neglected, in dealing with black educational needs.

(A) Steeger, Hanry. *You can remake America.* **Doubleday, 1968.**
The author is a former president of the Urban League. He offers specific information and proposals for improving the economic, educational and health condition of Negroes, chiefly by local means.

(A) Stone, Chuck. *Black political power in America.* **Bobbs, 1968. Paper.**
A rather journalistic and often witty survey of the Negro in our political system, with a sympathetic point-of-view.

(A) Stone, Chuck. *Tell it like it is.* **Trident, 1967. Paper.**
A collection of newspaper columns written by Stone for three Negro papers in the early 1960's. The writing is witty, personal and often caustic. Well worth reading.

(A) Sullivan, Leon H. *Build, brother, build.* **Macrae Smith, 1969.**
A noted Philadelphia black clergyman describes his projects and theories for getting Negroes successfully involved in the American capitalist system.

(A) Taeuber, Karl E. and Alma. *Negroes in cities; residential segregation and neighborhood change.* **Aldine, 1965. Paper.**
For adult background and research.

(A) Thurman, Howard. *The luminous darkness.* **Harper, 1965.**
A study of the social effects of segregation; thoughtful and hopeful of the future.

(A) Toffler, Alvin (ed.) *Schoolhouse in the city.* **Praeger, 1968. Paper.**
An anthology of lectures and essays about the needs and possible solutions of educational problems in big city ghettos. For teachers and students of education.

(Y) Wade, Richard C. (ed.) *Negro in American life.* **Houghton, 1965. Paper.**
A junior-senior high school collection of readings from the writings of Negro authors.

(A) Wattenberg, William W. (ed.) *"all men are created equal."* **Wayne State Univ. Press, 1966.**
Consists of five lectures on the general subject of equality, which were given at Wayne. Speakers included John P. Roche, William O. Douglas and Adolf Berle.

(A) Weaver, R. C. *The urban complex; human values in urban life.* **Doubleday, 1964. Paper.**
Seven essays by a leading official in the field of housing and urban renewal.

(A) Weisbord, Robert G. and Arthur Stein. *Bittersweet encounter.* **Negro Univ. Press, 1970. Paper.**
Serious study of prejudice and racism between Negroes and Jews.

(A) Weltner, Charles L. *Southerner.* **Lippincott, 1966.**
Southern problems discussed by a Georgia Congressman.

(A) Westin, Alan F. (ed.) *Freedom now!* **Basic Books, 1964.**
An anthology of about fifty brief excerpts from as many writers and magazines, each giving a vivid picture of some aspect or event of the civil rights movement. Good for supplementary reading.

(A) Weyl, Nathaniel and William Marina (eds.) *American statesmen on slavery and the Negro.* Arlington, 1971.
Interesting collection of documents and statements by famous Americans. Particularly striking in showing how racist thought is inherited from notable sources.

(A) Whittemore, L. H. *Together; a reporter's journey into the new black politics.* Morrow, 1971.
The author describes his interviews and impressions after a tour of leading black areas of the country. Interesting reading.

(A) Wills, Garry. *The second civil war; arming for Armageddon.* New American Lib., 1968. Paper.
A reporter's detailed and vivid account of what he has found to be the causes of white-Negro antagonism. It is pessimistic and the author fears for the future.

(A) Wilson, James Q. *Negro politics; the search for leadership.* Free Press, 1960. Paper.
An adult study of black political participation in Chicago.

(A) Wish, Harvey (ed.) *The Negro since emancipation.* Prentice, 1964. Paper.
Excerpts from the writings of prominent Negroes, illustrative of the drive for racial assertiveness.

(A,Y) Wormley, Stanton L. and Lewis H. Fenderson (eds.) *Many shades of black.* Morrow, 1969.
Forty-two prominent Negro-Americans write their views on race especially for this collection. Good for any library.

(A) Wright, Nathan. *Let's work together.* Hawthorn, 1968. Paper.
The author is a moderate black activist. This book analyzes the situation in the United States, describing those problems which whites and blacks must work out separately and those in which they must cooperate.

(A) Wright, Nathan. *Ready to riot.* Rinehart, 1968.
A report on Newark, N. J., intended to show white leaders why and how they must help the blacks. A militant point-of-view predominates.

(J) Young, Margaret. *First book of American Negroes.* **Watts, 1966.**
Discussion of Negro problems, civil rights, etc. Middle school level.

(A) Young, Whitney M., Jr. *Beyond racism.* **McGraw, 1968. Paper.**
Valuable discussion of the causes and extent of racism, and of what America can do to eradicate it. Good for any adult reader.

(A) Young, Whitney M., Jr. *To be equal.* **McGraw, 1964. Paper.**
A good statement by the late director of the National Urban League about the black people's future. It is not enough, he says, to eliminate injustice and discrimination. Both whites and blacks must make positive steps to close the gap created by the years.

(A) Zinn, Howard. *The Southern mystique.* **Knopf, 1964.**
The author is a white professor in a Southern college, and an active worker in the civil rights movement. This book is largely an account and analysis of the Southern reaction to the movement as he saw it. His principal thesis is that Northern and Southern whites have much the same prejudices; the South merely has an exaggerated version of them.

PART IV

NEGRO CULTURE — LITERATURE, MUSIC, THE ARTS

(A) Abraham, W. E. *The mind of Africa.* Univ. of Chicago Press, 1962. Paper.
The author is a Ghanian scholar. Here he compares the philosophy of African peoples with that in other societies.

(A) Abramson, Doris E. *Negro playwrights in the American theatre, 1925-1969.* Columbia Univ. Press, 1969.
A scholarly, thorough and well-researched study of twenty Broadway and off-Broadway dramas by Negro authors. The best existing study of Negro drama.

(Y) Adoff, Arnold (ed.) *Black out loud.* Macmillan, 1970.
Collection of sixty-some poems by black poets, chosen specifically for young readers of secondary school age. The general tone is primarily pride in being black.

(A,Y) Adoff, Arnold (ed.) *I am the darker brother.* Macmillan, 1968.
Sixty-four selections from twenty-eight American Negro poets, seeking to interpret the Negro's concept of his place in America. Good for high school or public libraries, or for use in English courses.

(A) Barbour, Floyd B. (ed.) *The black Seventies.* Sargent, 1970. Paper.
A collection of about thirty previously unpublished essays on the black experience in the arts, religion and other aspects of cultural life, projected into the future.

(A) Bernard, Jessie. *Marriage and family among Negroes.* Prentice, 1965. Paper.
Sociological study of Negro family life; useful for research.

(A) Billingsley, Andrew and Amy. *Black families in white America.*
Prentice, 1968. Paper.
Sociological study, depicting various levels of Negro family life.

(A) Bone, Robert A. *The Negro novel in America.* Yale Univ. Press,
1965 (rev. ed.) Paper.
History and critique of Negro literature, with biographical descriptions of the writers and analyses of their work. Useful for
teachers of black studies courses.

(A,Y) Bontemps, Arna (ed.) *American Negro poetry.* Hill & Wang,
1963. Paper.
Good anthology of fifty-six Negro writers.

(Y,J) Bradley, Duane. *Meeting with a stranger.* Lippincott, 1964.
An American and an Ethiopian boy each learns of the other's culture.

(A) Bronz, Stephen H. *Roots of Negro social consciousness.* Libra, 1964.
Paper.
About James Weldon Johnson, Countee Cullen and Claude
McKay.

(A,Y) Brooks, Charlotte (ed.) *The outnumbered.* Dell, 1967. Paper.
An anthology of stories, essays and poetry about minorities by
famous writers — Steinbeck, Saroyan, Baldwin, Benet and others.

(A,Y) Brown, S. A., A. P. Davis and Ulysses Lee (eds.) *The Negro
caravan.* Arno, 1969.
A thousand-page anthology of Negro writing prior to 1940, divided into eight types. Very useful to teachers as supplementary
material to black studies.

(Y,J) Brown, Vashti, and Jack. *Proudly we hail.* Houghton, 1968.
Twenty simply-told stories about Negroes for slow readers, grades
7-12.

(A) Butcher, Margaret. *The Negro in American culture.* Knopf, 1956.
Describes Negro contributions in music, theatre and the arts.

87

(A,Y) Chapman, Abraham (ed.) *Black voices.* New American Lib., 1968. Paper.
A seven hundred page anthology of writing by Negro authors; Wright, Bontemps, Hughes, many more.

(A,Y) Clarke, John H. (ed.) *American Negro short stories.* Hill & Wang, 1966.
Good collection for school libraries.

(A) Culp, Daniel W. (ed.) *Twentieth century Negro literature.* Arno, 1969. (reprint of 1902 edition.)

(A) Cunard, Nancy (ed.) *Negro.* Ungar, 1970.
An anthology of 460 pages, originally published in 1934, now reprinted when the original became a collector's item. Very complete, highly pro-Negro.

(A) David, Jay (ed.) *Black joy.* Cowles, 1971.
An anthology of black writings, extolling the pride of being black.

(A,Y) Davis, Charles T. and Daniel Walden (eds.) *On being black.* Fawcett, 1970. Paper.
Anthology of black writings, both fiction and non-fiction. Good supplementary reading for high school classes or above.

(Y) Dover, Cedric. *American Negro art.* N. Y. Graphic, 1960. Paper.
Excellent supplementary book for schools. It is about half text and half reproductions of many types of art by black artists.

(A) Emanuel, John A. and Theodore Gross (eds.) *Dark symphony.* Free Press, 1968. Paper.
Anthology of black literature, with a good bibliography.

(A) Gayle, Addison, Jr. (ed.) *The black esthetic.* Doubleday, 1970.
Essays relating to black creativeness in the fields of music, drama, poetry and fiction.

(A) Gayle, Addison, Jr. (ed.) *Bondage, freedom and beyond: the prose of black Americans.* Doubleday, 1971. Paper.
Short anthology of writings on Negro subjects.

(A) Gibson, Donald B. (ed.) *Five black writers.* N. Y. Univ. Press, 1970. Paper.
Essays by various writers about Wright, LeRoi Jones, Ellison, Hughes and Baldwin.

(A) Goldstein, Rhoda L. (ed.) *Black life and culture in the United States.* Crowell, 1971. Paper.
A useful anthology of essays for teachers and others.

(A,Y) Gross, Seymour and John E. Hardy (eds.) *Images of the Negro in American literature.* Univ. of Chicago Press, 1966. Paper.
An anthology of essays.

(Y,J) Halliburton, Warren J. and Mauri Pelkonen (eds.) *New worlds of literature.* Harcourt, 1970.
Anthology of writing by or about minority groups, adapted for slow high school readers. Includes an excellent teachers' guide.

(A) Hatch, James V. *Black image on the American stage; a bibliography of plays and musicals, 1770-1970.* BOS Publications, 1970.
Lists stage productions which involve blacks as playwrights, performers or as the subject of the production.

(Y) Hayden, Robert (ed.) *Kaleidoscope; poems by American Negro poets.* Harcourt, 1967. Paper.
An anthology of poetry by the most noted Negro poets. Good for use in black studies and literature classes.

(A) Hill, Herbert (ed.) *Anger and beyond; the Negro writer in the United States.* Harper, 1966. Paper.
Collection of essays by Negro writers on Negro writing, past and potential.

(A,Y) Hill, Herbert (ed.) *Soon, one morning; new writing by American Negroes, 1940-1962.* Knopf, 1963.
Essays, poetry, fiction. Useful for teachers as supplementary material.

(A) Huggins, Nathan. *Harlem Renaissance.* Oxford Univ. Press, 1971.
A valuable and thorough study of black creative culture in the 1920's, when many of the finest writers, artists and musicians flourished.

(A) Hughes, Langston (ed.) *An African treasury.* Pyramid, 1960. **Paper.**
Anthology of articles, essays, stories and poetry written by black African authors. Interesting selection.

(A,Y) Hughes, Langston (ed.) *Best short stories by Negro writers; an anthology from 1809 to the present.* Little, 1967. **Paper.**

(A) Hughes, Langston. *The ways of white folks.* Knopf, 1934; **Vantage paper reprint, 1971.**
Fourteen short stories on the black-white relationship.

(A,Y) Hughes, Langston and Arna Bontemps (eds.) *The poetry of the Negro, 1746-1970; an anthology.* Doubleday, 1970. **(rev. ed.)**
A large collection of poems written by blacks, and by white poets about blacks. Nearly six hundred pages long, it is an excellent library resource.

(A,Y) Hughes, Langston and Milton Meltzer. *Black magic; a pictorial history of the Negro in American entertainment.* **Prentice, 1967.**
A large, profusely illustrated book. From minstrels to modern music, theatre and movies.

(A) Kardiner, Abram and Lionel Ovesey. *The mark of oppression.* **World, 1962. Paper (copyrighted in 1951).**
Subtitled "Explorations in the personality of the American Negro," this is a serious sociological study, with cases. Useful for research on Negro culture and thought.

(A) Koblitz, Minnie W. *The Negro in schoolroom literature.* **Center for Urban Education, 1967.**
Subtitle: "resource materials for the teacher of kindergarten through the sixth grade."

(Y) Lindenmeyer, Otto. *Black history.* Avon, 1970. **Paper.**
High school level book derived from a TV show called "Black History: Lost, Stolen or Strayed," for which Lindenmeyer was a consultant. Covers mostly social and entertainment black history.

(A,Y) Lomax, Alan and Raoul Abdul (comps.) *3000 years of black poetry; an anthology.* Dodd, 1970. **Paper.**
An anthology of poems by black writers, covering many countries and thirty centuries. Good supplementary reading.

(A) Margolies, Edward. *Native sons; a critical study of twentieth century Negro American authors.* Lippincott, 1968. **Paper.**
A good scholarly critique of a number of Negro writers, whose work stressed the tragedy of Negro life in a white world.

(A) McCall, Dan. *The example of Richard Wright.* Harcourt, 1969. **Paper.**
A critical study of Wright's works. Useful for adult literary analysis.

(Y) Mirer, Martin (ed.) *Modern black stories.* Barron's Educational Series, 1971. **Paper.**
A dozen short stories by the best Negro authors. The book is intended for secondary school use and each story is accompanied by explanatory notes and study helps.

(A) Mitchell, Loften. *Black drama; the story of the American Negro in the theatre.* Hawthorn, 1967.

(J) Neurath, Marie. *They lived like this in ancient Africa.* Watts, 1967.
An elementary text on the cultures of old Africa.

(A,Y) Olson, Jack. *The black athlete.* Time, 1968.
This previously appeared as a series of articles in *Sports Illustrated,* and shows to what extent the black athlete is still a victim of the color line.

(A,Y) Robinson, John R. *Baseball has done it.* Lippincott, 1964.
How blacks got into big league baseball, and what they have found. A highly interesting report by a courageous star, who broke the color line.

(Y,J) Rollins, Charlemae (comp.) *Christmas gif'; an anthology of Christmas poems, songs and stories, written by and about Negroes.* Follett, 1963.

(A,Y) Sochen, June (ed.) *The black man and the American dream.* Quadrangle, 1971. Paper.
Anthology of essays and poetry by black writers dealing chiefly with the hopes and aspirations of Negroes in the first quarter of the twentieth century. Suitable for secondary school supplementary reading.

(A) Southern, Eileen. *The music of black Americans.* Norton, 1971.
Good textbook, college course level, covering the history of music created or performed by Negroes in America. For reference, study or just reading.

(A,Y) Szwed, John F. (ed.) *Black America.* Basic Books, 1970.
Twenty-three serious but interesting essays on the general topic of black culture and of the Negro's reaction to it. Good for school libraries, or general reading.

(Y) Turnbull, Colin. *People of Africa.* World, 1962.
The cultural background of those parts of Africa from which American Negroes came.

(A) Turner, Darwin T. and J. M. Bright (eds.) *Images of the Negro in America.* Heath, 1965. Paper.

(A) Williams, John (ed.) *Beyond the angry black.* Cooper Square, 1966.
Anthology of essays and stories with a common theme — Negro frustration and anger.

PART V

AFRICAN BACKGROUND AND HISTORY, REFERENCE WORKS, AND MISCELLANEOUS BOOKS ON RACIAL PROBLEMS AND BLACK STUDIES

(A) Adloff, Richard. *West Africa, the French speaking nations.* Holt, 1964.

(A) Alexander, Richard D. *Management of racial integration in business.* McGraw, 1964.
A study of practices and recommendations for large businesses.

(A) Allen, Robert L. *Black awakening in capitalist America.* Doubleday, 1969.
A study of the place of blacks in a white business world. College level reading.

(A,Y) *The American Negro; his history and literature.* Arno, 1968-70.
A 141-volume set of works by a wide range of writers on Negro history and culture. An invaluable reference source for any library.

(A) Bailey, Ronald W. *Black business enterprise.* Basic Books, 1971. Paper.
Comprehensive source on black economic development in various ways.

(A) Banks, James A. *Teaching the black experience; materials and methods.* Fearon Publishers, 1970. Paper.
Highly useful resource for teachers dealing with black studies courses.

(A) Belasco, Milton M. *The new Africa.* Cambridge Univ. Press, 1966. Paper.
African states south of the Sahara.

AFRICAN BACKGROUND AND HISTORY

(A) Bohannon, Paul. *Africa and Africans.* The Natural History Press, 1964. Paper.
History and descriptions of Africa south of the Sahara.

(A) Brown, Douglas. *Against the world: attitudes of white South Africa.* Doubleday, 1968. Paper.
A study of apartheid and the white people of South Africa. For any general library.

(Y,J) Buckley, Peter. *Okolo of Nigeria.* Simon & Schuster, 1962.

(Y) Burke, Fred (ed.) *Africa: selected readings.* Houghton, 1968. Paper.
Collection of source readings on African history. For grades 7-12.

(A,Y) Burke, Fred. *World areas today: Sub-Saharan Africa.* Harcourt, 1968.
History and development of the region.

(Y,J) Carpenter, Frances. *The story of East Africa.* McCormick-Mathers, 1967.

(A,Y) Cartey, Wilfred and Martin Kilson (eds.) *The Africa reader* (2 v.) Random, 1970. Paper.
Good background for teachers or students. Vol. 1 deals with the African colonial experience, vol. 2 with the modern situation.

(J) Chijioke, F. A. *Ancient Africa.* Longmans, 1969.
Forty-eight-page elementary text booklet on history of early Africa. Well written with many good color illustrations.

(J) Chu, Daniel and Elliott Skinner. *Glorious age in Africa.* Doubleday, 1965. Paper.
History of the three empires of Ghana, Mali and Songhay from the 8th to the 16th century.

94

(A,Y) Clark, Chris and Sheila Rush. *How to get along with black people.* Okpaku, 1972.
Subtitled "a handbook for white folks and some black folks too." A kind of etiquette book on dealing with social situations involving whites and blacks. A useful guide with a light touch.

(J) Clements, Frank. *Getting to know Rhodesia, Zambia and Malawi.* Coward, 1966.
Elementary level; one of a series.

(A) Clift, V. A., A. W. Anderson and H. G. Hullfish. *Negro education in America.* Harper, 1962.
This is a collection of twelve essays by as many writers. It is an adult book, primarily for teachers and others concerned with the history and problems of the topic. Especially useful is an article on administrators' problems in public school desegregation.

(A) Cole, Ernest. *House of bondage.* Random, 1967.
Vivid account of the Negro's position in South Africa.

(A) Collins, Robert O. (ed.) *Problems in African history.* Prentice, 1968. Paper.

(A,Y) Cowan, L. Gray. *Black Africa; the growing pains of independence.* Foreign Policy Ass'n., 1972 (Headline Series, No. 210)
A sixty-two page pamphlet describing the social, economic and political situation today of the African republics south of the Sahara.

(A,Y) David, Jay and Helise Harrington (eds.) *Growing up African.* Morrow, 1971.
Thirty-five selections chosen from autobiographical writings or statements by persons who here recall their early days in Africa. All are modern, and very readable. Each selection has an editorial comment.

(A) Davidson, Basil. *Africa, history of a continent.* Macmillan, 1966.
A large, beautiful and expensive book, with good text and magnificent photographs. Describes the ancient civilizations of Africa.

(A) Davidson, Basil. *Africa in history*. Macmillan, 1969.
Authoritative overall account of Africa from earliest times to
modern. Very readable. Useful for teachers or for secondary
school research.

(A,Y) Davidson, Basil. *African kingdoms*. Time, 1966.
A popular-type form of his *History of a Continent*, much less expensive. Also covers the story of pre-colonial Africa. Illustrated.

(Y) Davidson, Basil. *The African past*. Grosset & Dunlap, 1967. Paper.
Anthology of writings about African history. Good introductions
to each item.

(A) Davidson, Basil. *The African slave trade: pre-colonial history, 1450-
1850*. Little, 1961. Paper.

(A,Y) Davidson, Basil. *Guide to African history*. Doubleday, 1965.
Paper.
A general survey.

(A) Davidson, Basil. *History of East and Central Africa*. Doubleday,
n.d. Paper.
Synthesis of the earliest history of these regions down to the
beginnings of European colonization. Bibliography and forty maps.

(A) Davidson, Basil. *History of West Africa*. Doubleday, 1966. Paper.
A history of the area from earliest times to European colonization.
Bibliography and maps.

(A,Y) Davidson, Basil. *Lost cities of Africa*. Little, 1959. Paper.
Authoritative account of early African culture. Good for teachers
or secondary schools.

(A) Davis, John P. (ed.) *American Negro reference book*. Prentice, 1966.
Good coverage of most aspects of Negro life in American society.
Nearly 1000 pages. Constitutes vols. 8-9 of the Negro Heritage
Library.

(A) De Graft-Johnson, John. *African glory; the story of vanished Negro civilizations.* Walker, 1966 (reprint of 1954 ed.) Paper.
A survey of ancient Africa as revealed by archaeology.

(J) Dobler, Lavinia and William Brown. *Great rulers of the African past.* Doubleday, 1965. Paper.
Stories of five important African rulers. Illustrated.

(A,Y) Drotning, Phillip T. *Guide to Negro history in America.* Doubleday, 1968.
A guidebook to geographical locations associated with individual Negroes in American history. Usually the places are marked in some way. This book is also published under the title: "An American Traveler's Guide to Black History."

(A) DuBois, W. E. B. *Black folks then and now.* Holt, 1939.
Essays in African history during the days of slave trading. It tries to destroy the myth that Africans had no worthy history.

(A) Ebony. *The Negro handbook.* Johnson Pub. Co., 1966.
A collection of miscellaneous statistics, reports and biographical information dealing with Negroes. Useful reference.

(A) Farley, Reynolds. *Growth of the black population; a study of demographic trends.* Markham, 1970.
Sociological study of population trends of the Negro race.

(A) Fellows, Donald K. *A mosaic of America's ethnic minorities.* Wiley, 1972.
A scholarly study of the various minority groups with useful facts, statistics and diagrams. The black minority is dealt with in the first section.

(A) Foreign Policy Association. *Handbook on Africa.* Foreign Policy Assoc., 1966.
Teacher's guide on American-African relations. Contains a bibliography of articles, books, films.

(A) Foster, Philip J. *Africa, south of the Sahara.* Macmillan, 1968.
Descriptive history, geography and culture.

(A) Frye, William R. *In whitest Africa.* Prentice, 1968.
Written by a noted journalist, this is a good study of apartheid
and racial policy in South Africa, warning strongly of the dangers
to come.

(A) Gardner, Brian. *The African dream.* Putnam, 1970.
Perhaps the most useful and readable single volume describing the
whole history of British imperial administration in its African
colonies during the 19th and 20th centuries.

(A) Glazer, Nathan and Daniel Moynihan. *Beyond the melting pot.*
M.I.T. Press and Harvard Univ. Press, 1963. Paper.
Studies of the five largest ethnic minority groups in New York
City: Negroes, Puerto Ricans, Jews, Italians and Irish.

(A) Hallett, Robin. *Africa to 1875.* Univ. of Michigan Press, 1970.
A scholarly and serious history. Good background reading for
black studies courses, or for general information.

(A) Harris, Marvin. *Patterns of race in the Americas.* Walker, 1964.
A study of race relations in Latin America, by a Columbia University anthropologist.

(A) Hatch, John. *Tanzania, a profile.* Praeger, 1972.
Interesting 200-page history of this country. Good for general
reading.

(A) Jackson, John C. *Introduction to African civilizations.* University
Books, 1970.
History of early black Africa and its part in civilization.

(A) Jaffe, A. J. *Negro higher education in the 1960's.* Praeger, 1968.
Primarily useful as a reference source, this is a statistical and
evaluative study of some hundred colleges, chiefly for Negroes and
located in the South.

(A) Keesing's Research Report. *Race relations in the U.S.A., 1954-1968.* Scribner, 1970.
Valuable reference book for all libraries. Describes, outlines, summarizes all important matters under the title.

(A) Larson, Richard (ed.) *I have a kind of fear.* Quadrangle, 1970.
A collection of white teachers' diaries and statements, and black student essays and poems, reflecting their opinions of ghetto education. Useful reading for new teachers.

(A) Lewis, Roy and Yvonne Foy. *Painting Africa white; the human side of British colonialism.* Universe Books, 1970.
A lavishly illustrated book explaining how British administrators impressed their standards and culture on their African colonies. Good reading for historical background.

(J) McKown, Robin. *The republic of Zaire.* Watts, 1972.
A brief attractive history and description of this independent portion of what was once the Belgian Congo. Well illustrated and written for middle elementary grades.

(A) McPherson, *et al.* (comps.) *Blacks in America; bibliographical essays.* Doubleday, 1971.
Guide to the literature on Negro Americans. For black studies courses.

(A) Miller, Charles. *The lunatic express; an entertainment in imperialism.* Macmillan, 1970.
An interesting account of British involvement in East Africa before World War I, dealing especially with the remarkable feat of building a railroad from Mombasa to Uganda against incredible odds.

(A) Miller, Elizabeth. *The Negro in America: a bibliography.* Harvard Univ. Press, 1966.
This is a scholarly compilation and includes magazine articles. Most items are not annotated.

(A) Montague, Ashley (ed.) *The concept of race.* Crowell-Collier, 1964. Paper.
Reprints of valuable scientific essays which unite in rejecting the whole idea of race.

(Y) Morsbach, Mabel. *The Negro in American life.* **Harcourt, 1966. Paper.**

A 240-page overview of Negro history prepared for use in the secondary schools of Cincinnati and first published by the city's Board of Education. It is well-done, sympathetic, and non-controversial to an extreme. Contains many brief sketches of prominent Negroes.

(A) *The Negro and the city.* **(Compiled by the editors of** *Fortune* **from a special issue.) Time, 1968. Paper.**

Primarily a research and reference work with many tables and graphs. Much worthwhile information. Good for any library.

(A) *Negro in American history.* **3 vols. Encyclopedia Britannica Educational Corp., 1969.**

An extensive collection of writings and documents of all sorts, from Lincoln's Emancipation Proclamation to a defense of the KKK by its head. Vol. 1: 1928-1968; Vol. 2: 1854-1927; Vol. 3, 1567-1854. Valuable reference resource for any library.

(A) New Jersey Library Association. *New Jersey and the Negro; a bibliography, 1715-1966.* **NJLA, 1967.**

(A) New York City Board of Education. *Negro in American history.* **N.Y.C. Board of Education, 1964.**

A teachers' guide.

(A) Okoye, Felix N. *American image of Africa: myth and reality.* **Black Academy Press, 1971.**

Deals with common myths about Africa and how they persist. Has good bibliography.

(A,Y) Oliver, Roland and Caroline. *Africa in the days of exploration.* **Prentice, 1965. Paper.**

Collection of descriptions of Africa before European colonization, told by contemporaries. Suitable for any school library.

(A) Oliver, Roland and J. D. Fage. *A short history of Africa.* **New York Univ. Press, 1961. Paper.**

Resume of African history in 250 pages. Useful for general background reading.

(Y) Paradis, Adrian A. *Job opportunities for young Negroes.* McKay, 1969.
A useful handbook for secondary school pupils, guidance counselors, etc.

(A) Passow, A. Harry (ed.) *Education in depressed areas.* Teachers College Press, Columbia Univ., 1963.
Fifteen essays by leading educators on various problems of education for the disadvantaged, particularly Negroes. Serious and helpful reading for prospective and active professional educators.

(A,Y) Paton, Alan. *Cry, the beloved country.* Scribner, 1948. Paper.
Racism in South Africa.

(A) Paton, Alan. *The long view.* Praeger, 1968.
An account of the racial picture in South Africa.

(A) Pettigrew, Thomas F. *Profile of the American Negro.* Van Nostrand, 1964. Paper.
Very scholarly and valuable study of the nature of various behavioral traits of the Negro, as analyzed by scientific studies.

(A,Y) Ploski, Harry A. (ed.) *The Negro almanac.* Bellwether Pub. Co., 1971 (rev. ed.)
Very useful reference book of a thousand pages, containing historical, economic and political facts about Negroes: chronologies, statistics of many kinds, bibliography, etc.

(A) Pollock, N. C. *Studies in emerging Africa.* Rowman & Littlefield, 1971.
Serious study of sub-Saharan Africa with principal attention to geography and economic conditions. Reference or background.

(A) Porter, Dorothy (comp.) *The Negro in the United States; a selected bibliography.* Library of Congress, 1970.
Useful reference, especially in its listings of government and other public reports.

101

(A) Richards, Henry J. *Topics in Afro-American studies*. Black Academy Press, 1971.
Anthology of articles on black studies. Teacher background material.

(Y,J) Rollins, Charlemae (ed.) *We build together*. National Council of Teachers of English, 1967. Paper.
A reader's guide to Negro life and literature for elementary and high school use.

(A) Romero, Pat (ed.) *In black America: year of awakening*. United Pub. Corp., 1969. Paper.
This is a reference book and may be revised annually. Its nearly 600 pages in paperback contain a number of specially-written articles by various people on aspects of black affairs in 1968; lists of Negroes in official positions; and many other data.

(Y,J) Rottsolk, James E. *The story of Liberia*. McCormick-Mathers, 1967.

(A) Salk, Erwin A. (comp.) *Layman's guide to Negro history*. Quadrangle, 1966.
A general listing of books, periodicals and audio-visual aids on the subject.

(Y) Salkever, Louis and Helen Flynn. *Sub-Saharan Africa — struggle against the past*. Scott, Foresman, 1963.
Deals mostly with economic affairs. Secondary school level.

(J) Schloat, G. Warren, Jr. *Duee, a boy of Liberia*. Knopf, 1962.

(J) Schloat, G. Warren, Jr. *Kwaku, a boy of Ghana*. Knopf, 1962.

(A) Seligman, C. G. *Races of Africa*. Oxford Univ. Press, 1966. Paper.

(A) Singleton, F. Seth. *Africa in perspective*. Haydon, 1967. Paper.
General survey of present-day Africa.

(A,Y) Sloan, Irving J. *The American Negro; a chronology and fact book.* Oceana, 1965.
A brief book listing principal events in Negro history by years.

(Y) Thompson, Elizabeth. *Africa, past and present.* Houghton, 1966.
History of Africa from pre-historic times.

(A,Y) Toppin, Edgar A. *A biographical history of blacks in America since 1528.* McKay, 1971. Paper.
The first 200 pages comprise a good historical summary of black racial history in America. The latter half of the book contains biographical sketches of 145 prominent Negroes.

(A) Trubowitz, Sidney. *Handbook for teachers in the ghetto school.* Quadrangle, 1968.
Very readable book for teachers written by a Manhattan school principal.

(A) U.S. Bureau of Labor Statistics. *Negroes in the U.S.; their economic and social situation.* U.S. Gov't Printing office, 1966.

(A,Y) Van der Post, Laurens. *Heart of the hunter.* Morrow, 1961. Paper.
A book about the African bushmen, their culture, myths, and ways of life. Very well written, good for any secondary or general library.

(A) Ward, W. E. F. and L. W. White. *East Africa: a century of change, 1870-1970.* Africana Pub. Corp., 1972. Paper.
A history of the area, intended primarily as a text for African students, but of general interest to anyone. Contains maps.

(A) Washington, Joseph R. *Black religion; the Negro and Christianity in the United States.* Beacon, 1964. Paper.
A study of Negro religious thought and organization, holding that Negro churches are really religious fellowships, not a part of doctrinal, formal Christianity.

(Y) Welch, Galbraith. *Africa before they came.* Morrow, 1965.
Africa before the European colonial period.

(A) Welsch, Erwin K. *The Negro in the United States; a research guide.*
Indiana Univ. Press, 1965.
A bibliographic essay.

(Y) Were, Gideon S. and Derek A. Wilson. *East Africa through a thousand years.* Africana Pub. Corp., 1971. Paper.
A textbook for use in the secondary schools of East Africa. Covers the history of the area since 1000 A.D. Authors are teachers in Nairobi. Good writing and many maps and illustrations.

(Y) Williams, John. *Africa, her history lands and people.* Cooper, 1962.
Paper.

LIST OF PUBLISHERS

A

ABINGDON
Abingdon Press, 201 Eighth Ave., New York, N. Y. 10022

ADDISON-WESLEY
Addison-Wesley Publishing Co., Reading, Mass. 01867

AFRICANA
Africana Publishing Co., 101 Fifth Ave., New York, N. Y. 10003

AFRO-AMERICAN
Afro-American Publishing Co., 1727 S. Indiana Ave., Chicago, Ill. 60616

ALDINE
Aldine-Atherton, Inc., 529 S. Wabash Ave., Chicago, Ill. 60605

AMERICAN EDUCATION PUBLICATIONS
Xerox Education Group, Education Center, Columbus, Ohio 43216

AMERICAN HISTORICAL ASSOC.
American Historical Association, 400 A St., S.E., Washington, D. C. 20003

ANCHOR
See Doubleday

ANVIL
Serendipity Press, 1790 Shattuck Ave., Berkeley, Calif. 94709

APPLETON
Appleton-Century-Crofts, 440 Park Ave. South, New York, N. Y. 10016

ARLINGTON HOUSE
Arlington House, 81 Centre Ave., New Rochelle, N. Y. 10801

ARNO
Arno Press, 330 Madison Ave., New York, N. Y. 10017

ASSOCIATION PRESS
Association Press, 291 Broadway, New York, N. Y. 10007

ASSOC. PUBLISHERS
Associated Publishers, 1538 Ninth St., N.W., Washington, D. C. 20001

ATHENEUM
Atheneum Publishers, 122 E. 42nd St., New York, N. Y. 10017

ATHERTON
Aldine-Atherton, Inc., 529 S. Wabash Ave., Chicago, Ill. 60605

AVON
Avon Books, 959 Eighth Ave., New York, N. Y. 10019

B

BALLANTINE
Ballantine Books, Inc., 101 Fifth Ave., New York, N. Y. 10003

BANTAM
Bantam Books, 660 Fifth Ave., New York, N. Y. 10019

BARNES & CO.
A. S. Barnes & Co., Forsgate Drive, Cranbury, N. J. 08512

BARNES & NOBLE
Barnes & Noble, 105 Fifth Ave., New York, N. Y. 10003

BARRON'S EDUCATIONAL SERIES
Barron's Educational Series, 113 Crossways Park Drive, Woodbury, N. Y. 11797

BASIC BOOKS
Basic Books, 10 E. 53rd St., New York, N. Y. 10022

BEACON
Beacon Press, 25 Beacon St., Boston, Mass. 02108

BEHAVIORAL PUBLICATIONS
Behavioral Publications, 2852 Broadway, New York, N. Y. 10025

BELLWETHER
Bellwether Publishing Co., 167 E. 67th St., New York, N. Y. 10021

BLACK ACADEMY PRESS
Black Academy Press, 135 University Ave., Buffalo, N. Y. 14214

BOBBS
Bobbs-Merrill Co., 4300 W. 62nd St., Indianapolis, Ind. 46268

BOOKMAN ASSOCIATES
Twayne Publishers, 31 Union Square W., New York, N. Y. 10003

BRUCE
Bruce Publishing Co., 2642 University Ave., St. Paul, Minn. 55114

C

CAMBRIDGE UNIVERSITY PRESS
Cambridge University Press, 32 E. 57th St., New York, N. Y. 10022

CENTER FOR URBAN EDUCATION
Center for Urban Education, 105 Madison Ave., New York, N. Y. 10016

CHANDLER
Chandler Publishing Co., 124 Spear St., San Francisco, Calif. 94105

CHILTON
Chilton Book Co., 401 Walnut St., Philadelphia, Pa. 19106

CITADEL
Citadel Press, 222 Park Ave. South, New York, N. Y. 10003

CLARION
See Simon & Schuster

COLLIER
Crowell Collier & Macmillan, 866 Third Ave., New York, N. Y. 10022

COLUMBIA UNIVERSITY PRESS
Columbia University Press, 562 W. 113th St., New York, N. Y. 10025

CONCORDIA
Concordia Publishing House, 3558 S. Jefferson Ave., St. Louis, Mo. 63118

CONTINENTAL
Continental Publishing Co., 1261 Broadway, New York, N. Y. 10001

COOPER
Cooper Square Publishers, 59 Fourth Ave., New York, N. Y. 10003

CORNELL
Cornell University Press, 124 Roberts Place, Ithaca, N. Y. 14850

COWARD
Coward-McCann, 200 Madison Ave., New York, N. Y. 10016

COWLES
Cowles Book Co., 488 Madison Ave., New York, N. Y. 10022

CRITERION
Criterion Books, 257 Park Ave., New York, N. Y. 10010

CROWELL
Thomas Y. Crowell Co., 201 Park Ave. South, New York, N. Y. 10003

CROWELL-COLLIER
See Collier

CROWN
Crown Publishers, 419 Park Ave. South, New York, N. Y. 10016

D

DAY
John Day Co., 62 W. 45th St., New York, N. Y. 10036

DELACORTE
Dell Publishing Co., 750 Third Ave., New York, N. Y. 10017

DELL
See Delacorte

DELTA
See Delacorte

LIST OF PUBLISHERS

DEVIN-ADAIR
Devin-Adair Co., 1 Park Ave., Old Greenwich, Conn. 06870
DIAL
Dial Press, 750 Third Ave., New York, N. Y. 10017
DODD
Dodd, Mead & Co., 79 Madison Ave., New York, N. Y. 10016
DORSEY
Dorsey Press, 1818 Ridge Road, Homewood, Ill. 60430
DOUBLEDAY
Doubleday & Co., 501 Franklin Ave., Garden City, N. Y. 11530
DUTTON
E. P. Dutton & Co., 201 Park Ave. South, New York, N. Y. 10003

E

EERDMANS
Wm. B. Eerdmans Publishing Co., 255 Jefferson Ave. S.E., Grand Rapids, Mich. 49502
ENCYCLOPEDIA BRITANNICA
Encyclopedia Britannica Educational Corp., 425 N. Michigan Ave., Chicago, Ill. 60611
ERIKSSON
See Hill & Wang
EXPOSITION PRESS
Exposition Press, 50 Jericho Turnpike, Jericho, N. Y. 11753

F

FARRAR
Farrar, Straus & Giroux, 19 Union Square, New York, N. Y. 10003
FAWCETT
Fawcett World Library, 67 W. 44th St., New York, N. Y. 10036
FEARON
Fearon Publishers, 6 Davis Drive, Belmont, Calif. 94002
FOLLETT
Follett Publishing Co., 201 N. Wells St., Chicago, Ill. 60606
FREE PRESS
Free Press, 866 Third Ave., New York, N. Y. 10022

G

GINN
Ginn & Co., Statler Bldg., Back Bay P.O. 191, Boston, Mass. 02117
GLENCOE
Glencoe Press, 8701 Wilshire Blvd., Beverly Hills, Calif. 90211
GOLDEN BELL PRESS
Golden Bell Press, 2403 Champa St., Denver, Colo. 80205
GROSSET & DUNLAP
Grosset & Dunlap, 51 Madison Ave., New York, N. Y. 10010
GROSSMAN
Grossman Publishers, 44 W. 56th St., New York, N. Y. 10019
GROVE
Grove Press, 53 E. 11th St., New York, N. Y. 10003

H

HARCOURT
Harcourt Brace Jovanovich, 757 Third Ave., New York, N. Y. 10017
HARPER
Harper & Row Publishers, Keystone Industrial Park, Scranton, Pa. 18512
HARPERS MAGAZINE PRESS
Harpers Magazine Press, 2 Park Ave., New York, N. Y. 10016

HARVARD
Harvard University Press, Kittridge Hall, 79 Garden St., Cambridge, Mass. 02138
HAWTHORN
Hawthorn Books, 70 Fifth Ave., New York, N. Y. 10011
HAYDEN
Hayden Book Co., 116 W. 14th St., New York, N. Y. 10011
HEATH
D. C. Heath Co., 125 Spring St., Lexington, Mass. 02173
HELICON
Helicon Press, 1120 N. Calvert St., Baltimore, Md. 21202
HILL & WANG
Hill & Wang, 72 Fifth Ave., New York, N. Y. 10011
HOLT
Holt, Rinehart & Winston, 383 Madison Ave., New York, N. Y. 10017
HOUGHTON
Houghton Mifflin & Co., 2 Park St., Boston, Mass. 02107

I

INDIANA UNIVERSITY PRESS
Indiana University Press, Tenth and Morton Sts., Bloomington, Ind. 47401
INTERNATIONAL PUBLISHERS
International Publishers, 381 Park Ave. South, New York, N. Y. 10016

J

JOHNS HOPKINS PRESS
Johns Hopkins Press, Baltimore, Md. 21218
JOHNSON PUB. CO.
Johnson Publishing Co., 1135 "R" St., Lincoln, Neb. 68508
JUDSON
Judson Press, Valley Forge, Pa. 19481

K

KENNIKAT
Kennikat Press, 215 Main St., Box 270, Port Washington, N. Y. 11050
KNOPF
Alfred A. Knopf, 501 Madison Ave., New York, N. Y. 10022

L

LERNER
Lerner Publications, 241 First Ave. N, Minneapolis, Minn. 55401
LIBRA
Libra Publishers, 391 Willets Road, Roslyn Heights, N. Y. 11577
LIBRARY OF CONGRESS
Library of Congress, Washington, D. C. 20540
LIPPINCOTT
J. B. Lippincott Co., E. Washington Square, Pihladelphia, Pa. 19105
LITTLE
Little, Brown & Co., 34 Beacon St., Boston, Mass. 02106
LONGMANS
See McKay, David
LOTHROP
Lothrop, Lee & Shepard Co., 105 Madison Ave., New York, N. Y. 10016
LOUISIANA STATE
Louisiana State University Press, Hill Memorial Bldg., Baton Rouge, La. 70803

M

MACMILLAN
Macmillan Co., 866 Third Ave., New York, N. Y. 10022

MACRAE SMITH
Macrae Smith Co., 255 S. 15th St., Philadelphia, Pa. 19102
MARKHAM
Markham Publishing Co., 3322 W. Peterson Ave., Chicago, Ill. 60645
McCORMICK-MATHERS
McCormick-Mathers Publishing Co., 450 W. 33rd St., New York, N. Y. 10001
McGRAW
McGraw-Hill Book Co., 330 W. 42nd St., New York, N. Y. 10036
McKAY
David McKay Co., 750 Third Ave., New York, N. Y. 10017
MERIT
Merit Publishers, 410 West St., New York, N. Y. 10011
MESSNER
See Simon & Schuster
MICHIGAN STATE
Michigan State University Press, Box 550, East Lansing, Mich. 48823
M. I. T. PRESS
M. I. T. Press and Harvard University Press, 28 Carleton St., Cambridge, Mass. 02142
MONTHLY REVIEW PRESS
Monthly Review Press, 116 W. 14th St., New York, N. Y. 10011
MORROW
William Morrow & Co., 105 Madison Ave., New York, N. Y. 10016

N

NATIONAL COUNCIL OF TEACHERS OF ENGLISH
National Council of Teachers of English, 1111 Kenyon Road, Urbana, Ill. 61801
NATURAL HISTORY PRESS
Natural History Press, 277 Park Ave., New York, N. Y. 10017
NEGRO UNIVERSITIES PRESS
Negro Universities Press, 51 Riverside Ave., Westport, Conn. 06880
NEW AMERICAN LIBRARY
New American Library, 1301 Avenue of the Americas, New York, N. Y. 10019
NJLA
New Jersey Library Association, c/o Trenton Free Public Library, 120 Academy St., Trenton, N. J. 08608
N. Y. C. BOARD OF EDUC.
New York City Board of Education, Bureau of Curriculum Development, 131 Livingston St., Brooklyn, N. Y. 11201
N. Y. GRAPHIC
New York Graphic Society, 140 Greenwich Ave., Greenwich, Conn. 06830
N. Y. UNIV. PRESS
New York University Press, Washington Square, New York, N. Y. 10003
NORTON
W. W. Norton & Co., 55 Fifth Ave., New York, N. Y. 10003

O

OAK
Oak Publications, 33 W. 60th St., New York, N. Y. 10023
OBOLENSKY
Ivan Obolensky, 1117 First Ave., New York, N. Y. 10021
OCEANA
Oceana Publications, Dobbs Ferry, N. Y. 10522
OXFORD UNIV. PRESS
Oxford University Press, 200 Madison Ave., New York, N. Y. 10021

P

PAGEANT
Pageant Press, 101 Fifth Ave., New York, N. Y. 10003
PANTHEON
Pantheon Books, 437 Madison Ave., New York, N. Y. 10022
PAPERBACK LIBRARY
Paperback Library, 315 Park Ave. South, New York, N. Y. 10010
PARENTS MAGAZINE PRESS
Parents Magazine Press, 52 Vanderbilt Ave., New York, N. Y. 10017
PENGUIN
Penguin Books, 7110 Ambassador Road, Baltimore, Md. 21207
PEACOCK
F. E. Peacock, 401 W. Irving Park Road, Itasca, Ill. 60143
PILGRIM
United Church Press, 1505 Race St., Philadelphia, Pa. 19102
PITMAN
Pitman Publishing Corp., 6 E. 43rd St., New York, N. Y. 10017
POPULAR LIBRARY
Popular Library, 355 Lexington Ave., New York, N. Y. 10017
PRAEGER
Praeger Publishers, 111 Fourth Ave., New York ,N. Y. 10003
PRENTICE
Prentice-Hall, Englewood Cliffs, N. J. 07632
PRINCETON
Princeton University Press, Princeton, N. J. 08540
PUBLIC AFFAIRS PRESS
Public Affairs Press, 419 New Jersey Ave., S.E., Washington, D. C. 20003
PUTNAM
G. P. Putnam's Sons, 200 Madison Ave., New York, N. Y. 10016
PYRAMID
Pyramid Press, 820 Kentucky Home Life Bldg., Louisville, Ky. 40202

Q

QUADRANGLE
Quadrangle Books, 12 E. Delaware Place, Chicago, Ill. 60611

R

RAMPARTS
Ramparts Press, 2512 Grove St., Berkeley, Calif. 94704
RAND McNALLY
Rand McNally & Co., Box 7600, Chicago, Ill. 60680
RANDOM
Random House, 201 E. 50th St., New York, N. Y. 10022
READERS PRESS
Readers Press, 130 Bristol St., New Haven, Conn. 06511
REGNERY
Henry Regnery Co., 114 W. Illinois St., Chicago, Ill. 60610
REILLY & LEE
See Regnery, Henry
RINEHART
See Holt
ROWMAN & LITTLEFIELD
Rowman & Littlefield, 67 Adams Drive, Totowa, N. J. 07512
RUSSELL
Russell & Russell Publishers, 122 E. 42nd St., New York, N. Y. 10017
RUTGERS
Rutgers University Press, 30 College Ave., New Brunswick, N. J. 08903

LIST OF PUBLISHERS

S

SAGE
Sage Publications, 257 S. Beverly Drive, Beverly Hills, Calif. 90212

ST. MARTINS
St. Martins Press, 175 Fifth Ave., New York, N. Y. 10010

SARGENT
Porter Sargent, 11 Beacon St., Boston, Mass. 02108

SCHOCKEN
Schocken Books, 67 Park Ave., New York, N. Y. 10016

SCOTT FORESMAN
Scott Foresman & Co., 1900 E. Lake Ave., Glenview, Ill. 60025

SCRIBNER
Charles Scribner's Sons, 597 Fifth Ave., New York, N. Y. 10017

SEABURY
Seabury Press, 815 Second Ave., New York, N. Y. 10017

SHEED & WARD
Sheed & Ward, 64 University Place, New York, N. Y. 10003

SIMON & SCHUSTER
Simon & Schuster, 610 Fifth Ave., New York, N. Y. 10020

SLOANE
William Sloane Associates (See Morrow)

SMITH, PETER
Peter Smith, 6 Lexington Ave., Gloucester, Mass. 01930

SOUTHERN ILLINOIS UNIV.
Southern Illinois University Press, Lafferty Road, Carbondale, Ill. 62901

SOUTHERN METHODIST UNIV.
Southern Methodist University Press, Dallas, Texas 75222

STANFORD UNIV.
Stanford University Press, Stanford, Calif. 94305

STATE HISTORICAL SOCIETY OF WISCONSIN
State Historical Society of Wisconsin, 816 State St., Madison, Wis. 53706

STECK-VAUGHN
Steck-Vaughn Co., Box 2028, Austin, Texas 78767

STERLING
Sterling Publishing Co., 419 Park Ave. South, New York, N. Y. 10016

STEIN & DAY
Stein & Day, 7 E. 48th St., New York, N. Y. 10017

T

TEACHERS COLLEGE
Teachers College Press, Columbia University, 1234 Amsterdam Ave., New York, N. Y. 10027

THIRD PRESS
Third Press, 444 Central Park W., New York, N. Y. 10025

TIME-LIFE
Time-Life Books, Time & Life Bldg., New York, N. Y. 10020

TRIDENT
See Simon & Schuster

TWAYNE
Twayne Publishers, 31 Union Square W., New York, N. Y. 10003

U

UNGAR
Frederick Ungar Publishing Co., 250 Park Ave. South, New York, N. Y. 10003

UNITED PUB.
United Publishers Corp., 5530 Wisconsin Ave., Washington, D. C. 20015

U. S. GOVT.
U. S. Government Printing Office, Washington, D. C. 20402

UNIVERSE BOOKS
Universe Books, 381 Park Ave. South, New York, N. Y. 10016

UNIVERSITY BOOKS
University Books, 1615 Hillside Ave., New Hyde Park, N. Y. 11040

UNIV. OF ALABAMA
University of Alabama Press, Drawer 2877, University, Ala. 35486

UNIV. OF CHICAGO
University of Chicago Press, 5801 Ellis Ave., Chicago, Ill. 60637

UNIV. OF ILLINOIS
University of Illinois Press, Urbana, Ill. 61801

UNIV. OF KENTUCKY
University Press of Kentucky, Lafferty Hall, University of Kentucky, Lexington, Ky. 40506

UNIV. OF MICHIGAN
University of Michigan Press, 615 E. University, Ann Arbor, Mich. 48106

UNIV. OF NORTH CAROLINA
University of North Carolina Press, Box 2288, Chapel Hill, N. C. 27514

UNIV. OF OKLAHOMA
University of Oklahoma Press, 1005 Asp Ave., Norman, Okla. 73069

UNIV. OF PENNSYLVANIA
University of Pennsylvania Press, 3933 Walnut St., Philadelphia, Pa. 19104

UNIV. OF PITTSBURGH
University of Pittsburgh Press, 127 N. Bellefield Ave., Pittsburgh, Pa. 15213

UNIV. OF SOUTH CAROLINA
University of South Carolina Press, Columbia, S. C. 29208

UNIV. OF TEXAS
University of Texas Press, Box 7819, University Station, Austin, Texas 78712

UNIV. OF WISCONSIN
University of Wisconsin Press, Box 1370, Madison, Wis. 53701

V

VAN NOSTRAND
Van Nostrand-Reinhold Books, 450 W. 33rd St., New York, N. Y. 10001

VANTAGE
Vantage Press, 516 W. 34th St., New York, N. Y. 10001

VIKING
Viking Press, 625 Madison Ave., New York, N. Y. 10022

W

WALKER
Walker & Co., 720 Fifth Ave., New York, N. Y. 10003

WASHBURN
See McKay, David

WATTS
Franklin Watts, 575 Lexington Ave., New York, N. Y. 10022

WAYNE STATE UNIV.
Wayne State University Press, 5980 Cass Ave., Detroit, Mich. 48202

WEYBRIGHT & TALLEY
See Dutton

WHITE
David White Co., 60 E. 55th St., New York, N. Y. 10022

WILEY
John Wiley & Sons, 605 Third Ave., New York, N. Y. 10016

WILSON, H. W.
H. W. Wilson Co., 950 University Ave., Bronx, N. Y. 10452

WONDER BOOKS
See Grosset & Dunlap

WORLD
See Harcourt

Y

YALE UNIV.
Yale University Press, 92a Yale Station, New Haven, Conn. 06520

INDEX OF AUTHORS

INDEX
AUTHORS

INDEX
AUTHORS

INDEX OF TITLES

117

INDEX
TITLES

122